At Home with Decorating

Esther
Huntington
Reilly

At Home
with
Decorating

Chilton

Book

Company

Philadelphia
New York
London

ISBN 0-8019-5616-1 Cloth Edition
ISBN 0-8019-5625-0 Paper Edition

Manufactured in the United States of America by
Haddon Craftsmen, Inc.
Library of Congress Catalog Card Number 71-145803

Designed by Adrianne Onderdonk Dudden

Contents

To my helpful husband, Jim

⤳ **Preface**

Turning the Tables

As long as I can recall, I have read in magazines, newspapers and books, and heard on radio and television, that the American woman runs the household and holds the purse strings. In the field of interior decorating, that comment is as outmoded as the use of rushes on the floor instead of rugs. It may have been true in the 1930s, but something happened after World War II for which women themselves are to blame. When they left home for the factories and put the apron strings on their husbands, they forfeited their right to make the decisions for the purchases of home furnishings. A grave mistake it was because they lost their confidence, too. Yet in most cases the wife is not the artistic neophyte that her husband is. Her role in life is, after all, that of homemaker.

Some men have a superior sense of good taste compared to that of their wives, in which case it is right for the woman to take a back seat. In the great majority of cases, however, you as a woman are the one more suited for decorating the home because from the moment you first noticed the pretty colored dress on your doll you began to develop taste. When you and your brother were children, he played with toy trucks and glued airplanes together, while you kept changing your dolls' clothes and had fun arranging your dollhouse. During your teens, he eternally threw a basketball at the basket above the garage door or wrestled with his best friend, while you spent hours shopping for ensembles or made great plans to do your room over with Mother's help. All your life, you have been interested in what is pretty. Your brother and, later, your husband have been more interested in other things.

To start your marriage off right, you should know the precautions. It is your role, not your husband's, to decorate your new home. Don't even let the love of your life go with you to choose a pot holder. Don't get him started. If he insists on decorating, use a little female psychology. Take him shopping some beautiful fall Saturday when he planned to watch a football game on television. Jump right into the detail of everything. Go from store to store, introduce all sorts of pros and cons, run him ragged for three hours, purchase nothing, and top it off by getting him home too late to know who won the game. He may cool down so much that you will have the whole field to yourself. Another good idea to get him to lose interest is to buy a secondhand, black lacquered mahogany chest and insist you want him to refinish it in a light walnut stain. The job ought to tie him up in knots for weeks.

When a wife becomes pregnant for the second time, both she and her husband come down with a certain restlessness. Becoming dissatisfied with their apartment, they do not sit still until they have found their own house. Then the early marriage living room furniture is banished to the family room. So many wives at this point admit they do not understand how they ever could have purchased such ugly furniture. Actually, they didn't. They stood by, thrilled and dreamy-eyed, as their new husbands chose it. But when a couple moves into their first house, it is time to turn the tables. The woman's touch makes that house their home.

❧ At Home with Decorating

Good Taste

Educated and balanced human beings desire to improve their world and to live in surroundings that become more comfortable and beautiful as time passes. Thus we can see that the person with the responsibility for making the home inherits an instinct to improve its appearance as well as its degree of functional comfort.

In his attempt to live well, man creates much ugliness as a result of economic greed (polluted streams and air; cluttered, smoke-stained cities; bill-boarded and junk-lined highways) and much ugliness from poor taste (lines of ticky-tacky housing, incongruous architecture, gaudy economic symbols). No one means to be an agent of ugliness, but people inadvertently contribute to it through laziness, tolerance of filth, or ignorance of what is good taste. Laziness has to do with character, tolerance of filth grows from the environment, but good taste is basically an intellectual discipline that can be acquired through study, illustration and association. Good taste, then, is synonymous with a search for beauty and opposes what is ugly.

But here's the rub: recognizing beauty is one thing, creating beauty is another. Fortunately, most people have the basic values to appreciate balance, harmony, proportion, color, imagination, and spirit. Even though a person may not know how to achieve such a presentation in any of the arts, a room combining these elements is instinctively beautiful to him. Yet when we speak of beauty we are in the shifting sands of communication because "beauty is in the eye of the beholder."

Style and fashion introduce the element of time to beauty, and in relation to time these words date the elements that make up the good taste of any particular period. Things no longer in style or fashion are beautiful yet might clash with their present surroundings to produce a jarring note in a picture of which they are but a part. Imagine a woman, the exact copy of Marie Antoinette in hairdo and dress, going to a modern play as part of the audience! She would stand out like a sore thumb even though her beauty might be pleasant to the individual eye. Style, as viewed throughout history, operates between two extremes, a tendency to overdo and a tendency to be simple and severe. Between those two poles exists the ideal, the criterion of good taste. We never tarry with perfection; our collective desire is for innovation, since the pendulum of mode forever moves back and forth. In any case, no matter what the period, fashion must be followed to stay in tune with the times even though good taste may be somewhat sacrificed.

As intelligent human beings, we like to think that our individual good taste is the result of our own personality mixed with our ingenuity and creativity. If we study it carefully, however, we find that our personal style is closely tied to the characteristics of our times. This principle is difficult for some people to accept. They bristle in rage at the mention of style; I suppose they feel that they must be leaders, and to follow "style" would make them sheep. Nothing could be further from the truth because even a genius such as Michelangelo was the product of his period. His productivity was an accumulation of the best that the Renaissance city of Florence had to offer. Many influences on the style of any age are merely refinements of what has already been done in another age.

Because human beings are, for the most part, psychologically set in their habits and concepts, they seem to be limited to the established methods with which their physical natures have been involved. Thus, in order to show spontaneity, the field of decoration must swing from one field of expression to the other and back again. The rapidity with which we make these changes, interestingly enough, depends a great deal on world events. It follows that a thorough study of history often gives a clue to the decorations to be expected at the present and the road to be followed in the future.

Beauty, more than just a personal affair, becomes the outgrowth of the temper of an age. The top creators are not out of keeping with the time in which they live, but are part of and help to mold it. Their production controls the range of choice which helps to form the taste of any era, a segment of which makes up lasting beauty. Obviously, the average person has available to him what is produced at the time. Today's beauty is in good taste now. We can only wait for the future to tell us what turn our style is to take in the broad picture of man's creativity.

Good taste also consists of the best to be found in style, decoration's variable element. I firmly believe in following style because it leads us in fresh and vibrant paths of living; it moves us out of our ruts and permits us new emotions, pleasures and environments. Luckily for us, though, styles in home furnishings do not constantly change.

Who would have either the money or the time to be continually refurnishing her home? Yet there come the fatal moments when we must make purchases: the children have marked up the walls beyond toleration, the carpet is threadbare in the hall, the arms of the sofa have worn through to the stuffing, the drapery has faded, and last but not least you have built an addition to your house or bought a larger one.

It is a wise woman who at such times is aware of the latest style trends, so that her new investments will be in keeping for the years to come. To give an example of hitting an absolute low in taste: if Junior has bent one of your favorite lampshades, you would be foolish to replace it with a frilly early American one with row upon row of ruffles. This item has been off the scene for years. One would regret this purchase more and more as the years rolled by.

Out of Style

One of the most pleasant things about interior decorations is that you can refinish basic furnishings to suit new trends. A little paint, some new fabrics, and an updated arrangement can work wonders in a shell of a room and enliven its essentially well-designed furnishings. Obviously, you can't redo the style of a purse or an automobile, but with furnishings we are in no way forced to give up completely the items for which we have acquired a great fondness just because they are no longer chic.

Historically speaking, the home and its components are among the most slowly changing elements of our lives. For example, the Italian villages perched precariously on their hillsides seem out of keeping with the television antennas sticking up like weird modern sculptures on the roofs, and the honking, noisy cars rushing madly through the narrow streets appear to be the antithesis of the age-old buildings that time has forgotten. We are indeed quick to design an entirely new concept for an airplane, but slow to change the formula for a coffee table. The moral is that the human soul must have roots, and the home inevitably satisfies that need.

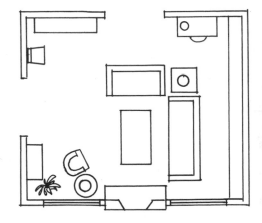

I welcome looking back to the past for inspiration in decorating as long as the past doesn't take over. We must adapt relics to suit our needs; otherwise, we are creating a stage upon which they sit waiting for the play that never begins. A home must be livable and useful, and items such as spinning wheels have no place in the twentieth-century home. What would your exclamation be if you came back five hundred years from now and saw an early electric sewing machine on display by the hearth? A lovely antique chest, however, with its warm patina glistening from years of constant rubbing and with drawers that work is an example of a relic that can be adapted to our use. No one as yet has improved upon the invention of the drawer for accessible storage space.

We should not revere an object just because it is old. It must have something else, or our home becomes more like a museum and we might as well put ropes across the rooms and charge admission. I can never forget one woman I met. So much did she treasure two ugly and uncomfortable Victorian chairs that she stretched golden cords from arm to arm over them, making it impossible for the poor

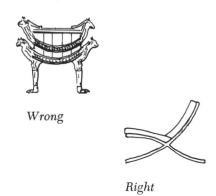

Wrong

Right

Wrong

chairs to serve their purpose. Her living room was little more than a display room.

Articles for the home come in two categories. Either they are useful or they have no purpose other than to delight the eye. If we bring the past forward, the object should be both useful and beautiful. If it is ugly, we might as well purchase one of the handsome, well-constructed pieces designed by today's top designers. The objet d'art, the accessory, cries out to be admired. To keep an ugly objet d'art would call for a great deal of sentimental value, or at least the knowledge of an extremely interesting story connected with it. Then even its unattractiveness would have a purpose persisting beyond its period.

When we can adapt antiques while surrounding them with the best that is offered us today, we are showing continuity and are thus not cutting off the past from the present. A home that combines the new and the old has priceless charm as well as durability. Yet this combination can be foolishly overdone. I once saw a huge, rough-hewn wagon wheel used as a focal point on a fireplace wall in an extremely modern home. Was it useful? Was it beautiful? Surely one cannot be sentimentally attached to a wagon wheel. The last item anyone's great, great grandmother would have saved from the trip across country in a prairie schooner would have been the wheel from the wagon. My fear was that it was so heavy that it might accidentally fall off the wall and crush somebody.

Basically, we wish to stay in style. We do so with clothes, automobiles, everything, in fact, including home furnishings, although here we tread more lightly. For instance, the number of people who have painted their living room walls white, the number-one wall color in the past decade, is overwhelming. It is likely that none of us would be at all challenged to duplicate the living room of our earliest memories. It would be far worse than last year's hat, and strangely enough, even though it was a chic room then, it would no longer appear to be in good taste.

Taste cannot be achieved without style. Our system of merchandising has accepted immediate style changes because items reflecting the latest design are available at once with all the information concerning them illustrated in brochures, magazines and trade journals. Even if you did decide not to follow the trend, who is going to manufacture the products of your imagination? I am not speaking now of any original type of accessory you may fashion with your hands, but the down-to-earth items you must have to make a house workable. Just picking a color that is out of favor can cause you so many unnecessary frustrations that you would probably give up in despair. We are influenced unconsciously by the trend of our times and we cannot avoid it. Happily, most of us have no desire to fight it. So let's relax and follow the best of today's style trends.

More than enough variety is offered to suit a tremendous range of tastes. By not going to extremes in expression, we can create something beautiful and pleasurable for our home. We mention not going to extremes in decorating because, unlike a dress that can be pushed to one side in a closet and forgotten, home furnishings are a long-term investment. You may go through many cars and live in several houses, but that sofa you thought was so smart and different fifteen years ago will probably still be sitting in the living room.

I must admit that good taste costs more. It is so much easier to decorate successfully with an unlimited budget than it is when each penny must be counted. High price and beauty are well married. May I extend my undying admiration to anyone who decorates well on a limited budget. There is a pet saying that is made innocently by one and all: "I can always pick out the most expensive thing." Naturally, you can. The most expensive thing is the best looking. But higher price does not necessarily indicate longer wear, more resistance to dirt and stain, or less fading. The truth is that a great deal of the time expensive articles may be less practical than their middle priced counterparts. But high priced items in general are outstandingly beautiful.

If you are limited by the amount of money you can spend and feel you need training, study all the high priced merchandize first and then determine to stay within your circumstances. This procedure helps you to eliminate crude color combinations and poorly designed pieces. A good rule to remember is this: *when in doubt, choose the simpler of two objects.* There is so much more room for error in elaborate pieces.

Top decorators have two qualities, imagination and good taste. Imagination is native, and no amount of education can impart it. It is a great gift that gives to life a thrill and satisfaction that almost nothing else can. Good taste is another element. Lucky is the person who is born with it, and he knows if he has it because all his life his choices and purchases bring delight to those around him or envy from those not near and dear.

One need not despair, however, if it is not his forte. Good taste can be acquired. Good taste rubs off, so become acquainted with it, surround yourself with it. Subscribe to the top decorating magazines; read, even take notes from, good books on antiques and decorating; look through the best furniture stores, decorating studios, antique shops, specialty stores and art studios. Go on open house tours through the wealthy homes in your community. When on vacation do not miss the old mansions open in almost every section of the United States. While you are looking at a room as an entity, remember to analyze the details that make up the room. Too many people haven't trained themselves to be observant. See movies that are noted for their outstanding backgrounds. Today, with exquisite colors expressed on film, viewing can be an overwhelming experience. Notice nature and what she does with color. Finally, take any decorating courses offered in your town. If all else fails, seek out the advice of a decorator who is known for her good taste as well as for her understanding of the individual. Blithely buying a rug because you need one does not constitute decorating. Much more is involved, including an understanding of the home as a whole.

The problem also involves personality. A good start would be to

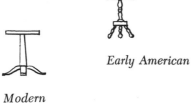

Modern   *Early American*

analyze yourself and your family. Your home should be a reflection of your personality and the tastes of your family. After all, the house is *your* workshop. Man may build houses, but woman creates the home.

The chances are that you have received an invitation to a home so different in personality from that of the hostess that you have been shocked. What are you really like: sophisticated, tailored, sweet, dramatic? If you are the dramatic type, handsome modern American furniture with sleek surfaces and vibrant colors would supply the type of background suitable for you. How silly you would look surrounded by Early American knickknacks! So use your personality type to carry out the theme of your home and it will appear integrated, pleasant and at peace with itself, with you and with your family.

Try to be sincere, but do it in good taste. What we are in our hearts, we show by the furnishings we display. It paints the picture. It cannot lie. You have all heard the expression too often that you know people by their friends. You also know people by what they choose to wear and by the way they decorate their houses. If a person is coarse, shallow, exhibitionistic, conceited, cold, sloppy or inconsistent, such traits can easily overcome the impression the home gives no matter how expensively it is put together.

Now that we have started on the road to self-analysis and self-improvement, let us pause and discover the little tricks in the trade that make homes livable. A home that is not livable is not a home at all, but just a house.

৯ 2

Livability

In our concern to make our homes beautiful, we often ignore the fact that the outside and the inside should be homogeneous. Since custom building is so expensive today, most of us find ourselves limited in our choice of design for the exterior of the house. Yet for the inside twelve styles are available to us in the selection of furnishings, or we can mix everything together for a delightful potpourri.

As a result, the lack of uniformity between outside and inside can sometimes be so drastic that it is somewhat like Greta Garbo taking a turn at being Mae West. It is shocking to pass through a doorway of a simple ranch house into a Louis XV decor, all white and glittering gold. If the lady of the house desires a French interior, she should certainly search for a house that has some semblance of a French exterior—long French windows on the front side, an elaborate double front door with curved moldings, and a mansard roof. Inside, the floor plan should be symmetrical, with a fireplace centered in the living room. With these few differences, some flow in temperament could be achieved.

The outside of a house should also indicate hospitality. One of the irritations, for instance, for family, tradesmen and guests is a lack of parking space. It is even more frustrating for strangers not to be able to recognize the position of the front door. This incomprehensible practice often occurs in our most contemporary architecture. Define the house's most important opening by a direct walk, correct planting or, if all else fails, a brightly painted door.

You should make a careful study to select the type of floor plan that

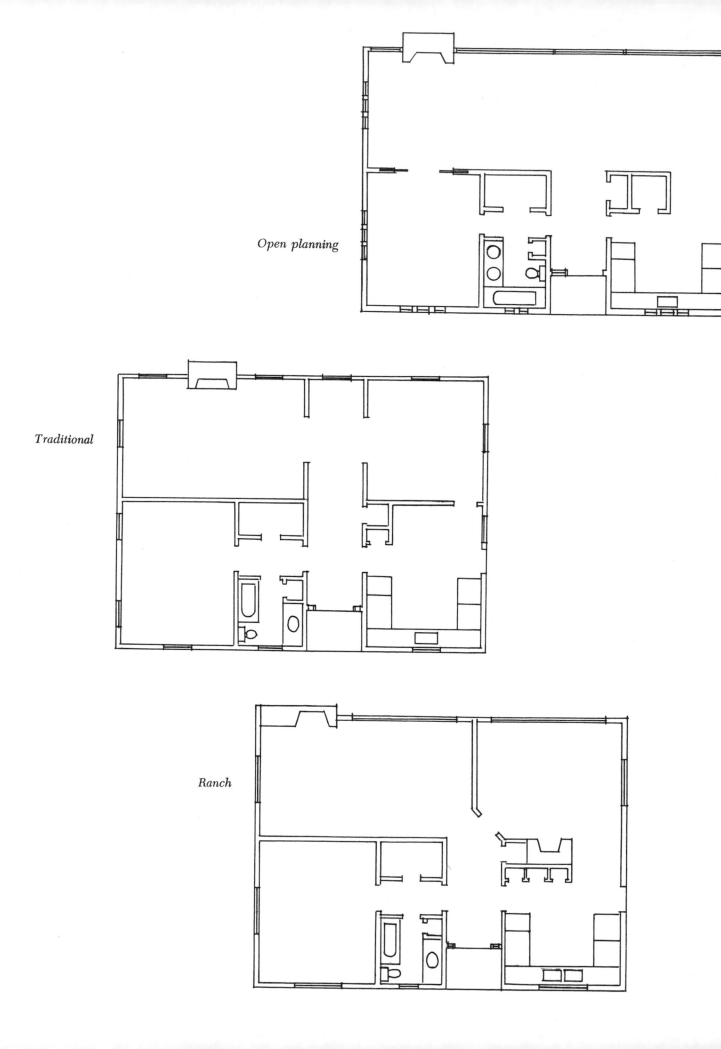

Open planning

Traditional

Ranch

provides the most beneficial type of living. Buying a house is a great investment, and the wrong choice could be disastrous for all concerned. Basically, you have a choice of two plans: one, the modern style of open planning that eliminates halls wherever possible, often has sheets of glass for walls, and incorporates a flat roof; two, traditional planning, in which rooms are entered from halls, windows are of normal size, and fireplaces are centered in rooms.

Today's preference is the ranch house that combines both open planning with sliding glass doors leading onto the patio in the kitchen-family room area and the off-center fireplace in the living room, but with halls leading to the main rooms, pitched roofs, and a compromise of large windows throughout the rest of the house. The plan is now so stereotyped and monotonous that it really behooves the homemaker to make a charming setting on the inside.

Let's see what living is like in open planning. Open planning is an answer for the introvert who is wrapped up with her family. By using this plan, although you may live in a residential area, the outside world can be shut out because many modern houses have no view out the front and the neighbors on the sides and back are excluded by a high fence. On the inside, the home is often built around an open court, or atrium, from which most of the house can be seen. But since halls and doors are at a minimun, there is little to shut off noise and vision.

What makes a home inviting and friendly? Number One on the list is probably the fireplace. The hearth is actually the center of the home. Even if you never burn a fire, the fireplace must look as if you do. Nothing can create a colder feeling than an empty fireplace. Blackened on the inside with soot, set up with logs and the necessary hearth equipment, the fireplace murmurs its pleasant greeting. The main object, though, is to use it during the correct months of the year. Nothing so warms and cheers the heart as a fire burning in the hearth. On the other hand, a constant view of a fireplace filled with ashes and crumpled paper is not pleasant. Only in the areas of the United States in which the summer months are too hot would I set up anything but logs in a fireplace. A hearth filled with potted plants or flowers may help take the mind off heat during those humid days.

The question of whether or not to paint the fireplace bricks constantly arises between husbands and wives. Beautiful, old brick should not be painted. It has mellowed through the years and its beauty must be seen. On the other hand, brick that has been manufactured to look old should be painted. It is an imitation—and it looks unreal. When in doubt, paint. Painted brick, although it need not be, is acceptable in all but the most tavern-like decor. Paint it, but choose a neutral color, preferably white, off-white, or pale gray if the walls and woodwork are gray; and when there is a mantle or not much brick showing, black is acceptable.

Fireplaces today are often considered such a downright bother by a number of housewives that they are converting to gas logs. Gas logs do not look, smell or sound like the real thing. They do give off heat, but furnaces are more efficient for that. I would rather see no fire at

Wrong

Right

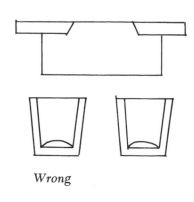

Wrong

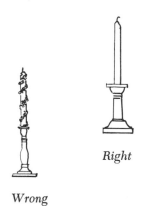

Right

Wrong

all than an imitation. I do not object to a gas outlet that helps to start a blaze. The convenience is worth it.

Some women are so enamored of fireplaces that they go to extremes and set up furniture right in front of the hearth as if the home were a cabin in the mountains and a skier's feet needed thawing out. A great deal of the time there is no fire, and to be positioned to stare at set up logs is not the ultimate activity in appreciation of beauty. Neither should chairs have their backs to the rest of the room when situated close to the fireplace. A room should to a degree open up to itself, not have tight little areas that shut out the rest of the room. As a final word, I pray that your contractor has been thoughtful enough to place the fireplace in the middle of the wall so that the furniture may be successfully arranged around it.

Candles, whether placed in candlesticks, candelabra, or sconces, warm a room psychologically. Do, though, light new ones and then blow them out so that the wick does not appear to be untouched. Even when they are not lit, candles suggest all sorts of delightful things. To quote Truman Capote: "Candles are magic wands; light one and the world is a story book." What can be more romantic than eating by candlelight during the dark winter months? Who can be disagreeable when surrounded by the soft light given off by candles? I do hope that you are eating the evening meal in the dining room so that this lovely background can be achieved. You simply cannot bring children up with excellent manners and a gracious attitude toward dining when they always eat in the kitchen.

Candles should be white or natural beeswax in an informal atmosphere. Maybe in another life and another world colored candles will be correct, but not in this one. I do not want to put the little old ladies owning candle shops out of business, but I wish they would concentrate on selling something else. A candle should not be ornate. It is a utilitarian item, and its purpose is to burn down. It functions just the way a light bulb does. I have not yet noticed any jewelled light bulbs. Only the candleholder is permanent, and it can be as decorative as you wish. One of my clients insisted on using bright blue candles in an elaborate gold sconce that was hung on a white brick wall. She felt that the white candles would not show up against the white wall. She was right, they would not, and that was the whole idea. The blue ones ruined the effect. Only on special holidays would I agree to using colored candles.

There are those who flood their homes with candlesticks with nary a candle in sight. It is a bit like having a lamp around without a light bulb. The only excuse for an empty candlestick is that the temperature has gone up beyond eighty-five degrees. Candles can't take the heat. Nothing strikes me quite so humorously as to come upon a candle that has had a heat stroke and is hanging limply over its holder.

Lamps, too, can be an asset or a detraction in terms of livability. There are probably more poorly designed lamp bases in this world than any other thing. Unfortunately, price is not always a criterion for good taste in this department, but it generally helps. The lamp base's function is to hold up a light bulb at the correct height so that anyone sitting next to it can read with ease. Some manufacturers appear to disregard this fact. Some lamps are such giants in height that they must sport monstrously long shades to prevent the light bulbs from glaring into the user's eyes. The bases themselves are anything from miniature spinning wheels to nude cupids eating grapes. It is asking a great deal for such bases to take on the extra burden of accepting light bulbs. And I do not even wish to discuss hanging lamps. I am allergic to them.

Tall lamps are waning in popularity. The height of your lamp depends on the height of the table on which it stands. Desks have somewhat low lamps, but tables, coffee table height, need tall ones. A good rule of thumb is to have an overall measurement of fifty-six inches, more or less, from the top of the lamp to the floor. This rule applies to floor lamps, too. It is effective for all the lamps in any room to be approximately the same height so that at night the lighting does not cause a roller coaster effect.

The job of a lamp shade is merely to cover that small light bulb enough to insure pleasant lighting. The shade needn't be three feet tall or odd in shape, and it is out of character when it is so elaborately decorated that it becomes too much of an attention-seeker. A frilly lamp shade about ready to dance the cancan is acceptable only in the boudoir. Lamp shades should be simple in shape and tastefully decorated without much more than a band, top and bottom. Be sure also that its shape is right up to date in style. Generally, shades should be a neutral color, white or off-white (the most acceptable), particularly when the shade is translucent. On an opaque shade, black, gold or silver can be smart in a sophisticated interior, and in some rustic decors dark green or dark red looks good, although even they may attract too much attention. Only in a fun kind of room should printed fabrics be used on shades. Opaque shades never give as much light as translucent ones.

Wrong

Right

Normal lamps with normal shades are items that add greatly to the pleasing atmosphere of a home. During the day we like our light clear and bright, but during the night we regress to our caveman days. Shadows create a cozy, shut-in feeling. Remember, then, to close those draperies at night.

Be sure your lamp shades are clean, fresh looking, and up to date. Look at them through the eyes of a stranger and see if they meet the test. You become so used to your own home you do not always realize when you have an eyesore. New shades may be needed. An attractive lamp base can go on forever, but it needs a new hat at least every ten years.

Now that window shades are back in favor, we must take stock of them also, for they often end up looking frayed and dirty. Old faded fabrics on furniture do not necessarily join the replacement category as long as they are clean. Faded fabrics often help create that delightful lived-in look that is impossible to duplicate with new fabrics.

Just as with colored candles, plastic flowers can destroy the warmth of a room. In one home, I counted eight bouquets of these tasteless creations in the living room. When I questioned the lady of the house

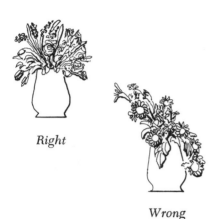

Right

Wrong

about having so many in one room, she answered that she loved flowers. She must have been a little mixed up. Man simply has not been as successful as God in this department. The fresh, the clean-cut quality (flowers wilt before they gather dust), the clear colors and the sweet fragrance of flowers cannot be duplicated by man. A bouquet of flowers arranged in a natural fashion can perk up the dullest room. Even in the most formal room, flowers are most attractive when they are arranged with a light hand, almost as if nature had done it herself.

Although some decorators believe that flowers should match the color scheme of the room, I for one do not feel that it is paramount. Nature renders matching difficult because she clearly prefers bright yellows, pinks, blues and lavenders in the spring, while the golds, oranges, and russets lead the parade in the fall. The startling contrast of a bouquet that is just the opposite of the color scheme of a room can give the right amount of lift and the impression of discord that the room needs. If your life is too busy to be constantly arranging cut flowers, potted ones are a good alternative. They last a long time, and nature conveniently does the arranging for you.

Growing plants are in the same catagory as cut flowers. Some plants grow in the shade, in a half-and-half situation, and some do best in the sun. Small potted plants are a delight, singly or in groups, and are particularly pleasant to see at a windowsill as the eye lifts from the inside to the outside. They may also rest in a plant stand on the far side of a long hearth, on a table, desk, chest, or even on the floor if enough plants are placed together to be effective. Large plants generally must rest on the floor and are the perfect answer to that

Wrong

empty space or to soften the angles of a corner. Huge plants are particularly suited for the contemporary house because they help correlate the indoors and the outdoors.

Plant care is minimal, but the subject demands understanding. Every decorator should recognize the beginning of the last stage in the life of every good house plant. That straggly plant must go. Some women, however, have such green thumbs that the plants react as if they were in the Amazon jungle and grow and grow and grow. As soon as the scotch tape comes out to help hold up the plant on its climb up to the second story, that one should go. You don't want to scare your guests half to death. Then there is the type of woman whose hopes

Wrong

far exceed the plant's abilities, and the poor little thing is swallowed up in a huge pot, drowned in a sea of dirt.

A nice touch in a living room is the appearance of fruit, nuts or candy. We can add books, magazines and newspapers to our list. Whole walls of shelves, combining books and objets d'art, possibly with cabinets below, radiate warmth and good fellowship. In the open-plan modern house they even make good wall dividers. Some people regard the living room as no place for such items, but I cannot agree. Let's make this room live up to its name.

The display of books and magazines reveals much about the inhabitants of the home, and the absence of such material discloses even more. This may be the age of television, but many of us would prefer the members of our family to read. One way to get them to read is to have books and periodicals readily available. Purchase a good book occasionally and make weekly trips to the neighborhood library in order to bring home as many books as the law allows. Read aloud to the younger members of the family as a regular bedtime treat. It will give everyone much joy. Add to the pleasure even more by reading in front of a fire buring brightly in the hearth.

Books naturally belong on bookshelves, but they may also be stacked on tables (the large library table is back again), desks, benches and stools—a trick that gives character to a room. For example, I remember a next door neighbor's living room during my childhood. In front of three small paned windows was a huge oak library table loaded down with books and magazines except for two fat, bottle lamps sporting pleated shades. On each side of the table was a large over-stuffed, but comfortable, Victorian chair slipcovered in bright flowered cretonne. It was the perfect place for a little girl to curl up and read to her heart's content.

A few books (those large, expensive volumes containing a ton of colored photographs, and nicknamed "coffee table books"), magazines and the latest newspaper are not out of place on the coffee table, even though it is dead center for our social life. The care of the magazines and newspapers is left strictly up to the homemaker. She must be on her toes not to allow too many periodicals to collect. No matter how good everyone's intentions are, you know that when the back numbers have been forgotten for the new they must be thrown out or carefully saved elsewhere.

The book stand is back again, a status symbol, yet certainly practical too because the family is much more likely to look up words in a five-pound dictionary if it is readily available. It can be a good-looking accessory as well. Another somewhat old-timer returning to our midst is the magazine rack. Although helpful, it can be a problem if not carefully tended; the old issues must be weeded out as soon as an overcrowded condition exists.

Magazine racks have at last found their way into the master bathroom, which has long been a favorite reading spot for some household heads. Although it does seem peculiar, we might as well accept the fact and play up to it. It does not need to be a conventional type of holder. You can improvise.

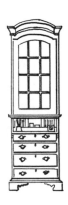

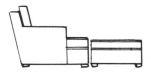

Desks are an attractive item to have in the living room, but not the big masculine, kneehole type. That belongs in the den or in the master bedroom. A desk in the living room is more decorative and is perhaps recognized more as a writing table, although it may have a few drawers. This is more or less your desk, helpfully situated away from the noisy area of the family room. Here, pens and pencils should be available, perhaps also containers for in-going and out-going mail, your favorite books and magazines, and handsome clock. Even an opened typewriter is acceptable if it is frequently used. Since it is *her* desk, here is a perfect location for a sentimental item or two, even photographs.

It was inevitable with the return to popularity of eighteenth-century furniture that secretaries would make their reappearance. They are admirable pieces because they help to break up the height line of furniture in the room. It is disheartening to learn how many women keep the drop-lid tightly closed and relegate the desk chair to the wall on one side. It is a dead giveaway of a wasted piece of furniture. So open up the desk area, put a chair or bench up to it, and let your secretary live a little.

No matter where the husband's desk is disposed of in the home, a handy filing cabinet should be close by, but hidden in a closet in any room but the den. A man likes to be able to put his hands immediately on any papers he needs in a hurry.

How important are comfortable, good-looking chairs! I am stupefied at the number of husbands who are hooked on the lounger chairs covered with plastic. Apparently, they have never tried a deep, tailored lounge chair with a separate back-cushion stuffed with down and a broad ottoman to match. This combination produces sheer comfort and is guaranteed to be the best place to snooze outside of bed. Although designers certainly have tried to make loungers look inviting, they still have a stiff, bulky look that cannot be disguised. They may not take up much room when closed, but they can grab space when open. An awkward room arrangement or at least a scarred wall behind the lounger may result.

I have never thought that plastic or leather is particularly soft and yielding. Plastic can be sticky in hot weather and is generally sloppy looking unless pulled tight over the stuffing. For practicality, it cannot be beaten, but I prefer a solid tweed underneath me for any long period of sitting.

Any large upholstered piece, especially the sofa, appears much more friendly with decorator's pillows on it. They are great answers for color coordination and can add to comfort, too. However, don't overdo it to the point of discomfort. Be sure that oversized pillows are used on deeper than normal pieces. When guests continually pull a pillow out from under them, it is time for that particular pillow to be retired.

A surefire way to achieve a high degree of ease is to purchase your upholstered pieces with the back and seat cushions made of down, which takes first prize for the lived-in look. In fact, down cushions manage to convey a feeling that lots of people were sitting in the room just a second ago. I have designed a rustic, masculine type of room with deep overstuffed pieces to which the down gave an appealing look. I have also seen formal living rooms that erroneously hinted that the lady of the house must be a sloppy individual. If you don't care for the lived-in look, stay away from down. Limiting the down to back cushions or using the down/spring combination for the seat generally achieves a happy compromise. The look is inviting without seeming unkempt.

Generally speaking, it is better not to place a sofa against a window wall. The sofa is number one when it comes to providing seating space in the living room, and since people like to look out of windows they are a little put to it if their backs are toward the only window in the room. In a ranch house, the architect often thoughtlessly places the only window, a picture window, on the only long wall. His mind must be in southern Italy, where shuttered windows prove that nobody wants to look out. Not so in the United States. You women who keep your draperies closed all day should bear that in mind. At night, it is quite another matter.

Another article that should be considered is the round, skirted table, a pet of many women for some time now. Material generates more warmth than wood, so a skirt in a luscious color can liven up a characterless corner or help distribute color more evenly around the room. It costs less than a good wooden piece the same size and can be a do-it-yourself project. What is hidden underneath hardly matters if the table is about twenty-five to twenty-nine inches high and thirty inches in diameter, and is sturdy. You can make it even jauntier by adding a contrasting trim around the bottom. If the fabric is white, you may want to be practical and add a glass top.

For children's and adult games, a table certainly is valuable. Because most games call for concentration and are basically quiet pursuits, I believe that a permanently set-up game table should be in the living room. There a chess or monopoly game need not be disrupted if it needs to be kept out for more than one sitting. If something like dominoes or bridge is the favorite, let the game stay in its box ready for use at one corner of the table.

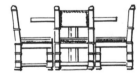

If the chairs of the game table are semiupholstered, they are a boon for that extra company for an evening of conversation, and they tuck away so easily when not in use around the table, sparing the living room from appearing to be all chairs. If some evening your children have all been invited out and you find yourself dining with only your husband, it is pleasant to change the scenery by using the game table as a supper table and eating in front of a fire glowing in the hearth. Truly, you cannot lose with a game table.

The mention of food brings to mind the mobile server. It is such a practical item that no hostess should be without one. It can be set up in the living room as a bar awaiting company, or it can come rolling in from the kitchen with coffee and refreshments at the right moment.

It would be difficult to speculate about living in a home without a picture hanging on the wall. Pictures make a room cozy. But don't use too many. And I am sure you have had the experience of framing a $2.50 print with a $40 collar. Framing is an art, and can make or break a picture, so you should be sure to have your work done at a framing shop known for its taste.

We have gone back to larger paintings lately, having developed a Texas attitude toward them. The concept is "the larger the size, the more simple, neat and sophisticated the interior." Yet it is no problem to combine large and small pictures in one room. You may

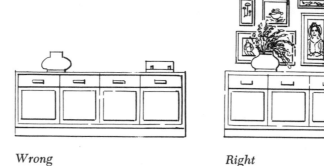

Wrong   *Right*

hang a large one over the fireplace and group smaller ones over the sofa. Never place a masterpiece or your favorite among an assortment of pictures. It becomes lost in the crowd. Like wallpaper, a group of pictures warms a room perceptibly. You can have matching prints all framed alike or a potpourri—each one different and in a different frame.

Pictures do not always need to be hung, but can lean against the wall from the top of chests or buffets. This contrivance may appear odd, but it is just one more little trick that contributes to a room's livability. I cannot condone, however, the peculiar practice illustrated lately in decorating magazines of leaning a picture against a lamp or using the back of the sofa as its stand. Clumsiness while turning on the lamp in the dark or falling awkwardly on the sofa are too common and make such perches precarious.

Wrong

Some couples are so egotistic about their paintings that they must show them off by placing a small light over them. Unlike museums, houses are usually supplied with adequate lighting so the picture lamps bespeak mere affectation.

Unframed mirrors are passé unless they occupy an entire wall space and thus become an architectural feature rather than a decorative one. A regular unframed mirror appears undressed and as archaic as grandmother's antimacassar. No need to give it to Goodwill Industries, though; just take it to a good framing shop and have it framed in a style matching your decor.

Right

A living room generally does not call for patterned wallpaper because it is already filled with items that attract attention, but if you have a hall, a bathroom, a kitchen, a dining room or a bedroom wall that is bare, try some wallpaper. If there is a question in your mind of whether to cover one wall or four (never two, and three only if one wall is paneled), the safe bet is to cover four. Then there is no hazard of creating an off-balance situation. Be careful about your choice of paper; if you are unsure of yourself, you can solve your problem by going to a store with an excellent reputation for good merchandise as well as for salespeople who care. There are some real horrors of papers on the market, often expensive and usually designed for commercial use. Still, price indicates variety, individuality and beauty. If you cannot afford hand-blocked papers, spend time studying them. You will be surprised how often a low-priced paper is almost an exact copy of a more expensive one. All papers can be vinyl-coated, so there is no worry today about their practicality. If you live in a tract house, wallpaper can give it distinction over those around you. So investigate wallpapers if you have not been using them up to now, and take at least several days to do it. There are literally thousands on the market.

Wrong

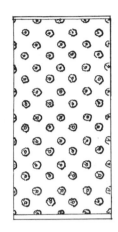

Right

Like large plants, screens also colorfully fill an empty corner. Too few women make use of a screen, an item that can be particularly decorative and beautiful. When one room appears to open out too boldly into another, a screen can break the line and also create a cozy corner. It can separate an area that needs to be defined and can be a joy to the eye. Why not explore the possibility of a screen by the kitchen door? Do not be mistaken. There is not a female alive who can resist peeking at the condition of your kitchen even during the most formal affairs. In any case, glance around your living room and dining room to see if a handsome screen could not add to the effectiveness of the atmosphere you are trying to fashion.

Music is an integral part of American living. Some husbands consider a stereo an absolute must, and insist that it be installed in the living room. I have seen living rooms set up practically like Carnegie Hall to ensure perfect reception. It is a crime when the social arrangement of a room is completely destroyed for one interest. Husbands must realize that other pastimes besides listening to music go on in this room.

A piano, from a grand to a spinet is a perfect appendage for the living room if you have room for one. Not, though, that old upright painted white. That is strictly a recreation room piece. If you must have it in the living room, though, by all means leave it in dark mahogany. You can successfully minimize its appearance by enclosing it within bookshelves. A piano with open music on its stand always gives people a genuine feeling of warmth and enjoyment.

A radio in the kitchen is helpful for those dull moments that cooking produces. The older children probably insist on one near their bedsides so they can listen to music at bedtime. I would suggest that you do not play music constantly in your home. It loses its punch that way. The American people are "musicked" to death today. We hear it so much in public that we do not even realize it is being played. It is just one more sound added to our already too noisy world.

Television may be necessary, but not in the living room. We calmed down after our initial excitement years ago over this amazing invention, and it did not take long for us to house it in the family room. That's where it belongs.

Since we are discussing livability, we must mention pets. They do a great deal to make a home pleasant. The tail-wagging dog who greets you happily at the door, the lazy cat who cuddles by the glowing fire, or the cheery notes of the canary that match the sunshine on a crisp day cannot be duplicated. I leave out fish. I place them in the hobby category. I have tried to love them, but there is nothing warm about fish, and the elaborate tanks set up for them seem artificial and noisy. I have never run into one yet that does not have an unpleasant, mechanical sound with its apparatus. As for you who allow your little boys to have boa constrictors for pets, we are not even on speaking terms with each other.

Sentiment need not be left out of the living room today, or indeed the whole house. Photographs have found their way back into the living room. One or two are fine, but I do not include in this group a picture of you in your wedding dress. I have never been able to understand why husbands must be repeatedly reminded as the years roll by of what cute chicks their wives used to be. Frankly, I would rather forget it, too.

In addition, small trinkets or mementoes from your past or from a trip work out well as accessories on a table. But do not lose sight of the fact that the living room is not a museum. If you have too many such items, the excess should be retired to the den or the master bedroom. A good idea would be to stow half of them on the third shelf up in a kitchen cupboard and every few months make a switch, a move that would delight your friends and neighbors. Of course, books and curios can share the same shelves in a bookcase, but remember that for a dressy room the effect is not formal enough. In this situation, the shelves should hold either objects or books, not both.

We have spoken of many ways to warm a room. Objets d'art often create still another feeling for a room. Reflected light adds to the gaiety of a room. Homes with accessories made of wood or wrought iron look dull, which is often an affliction of the contemporary home, particularly if the occupants have gone in heavily for Danish Modern.

It is perhaps easier to achieve reflection in a formal room because dressy objets d'art are composed of silver, gold leaf, brass, crystal, fine china, porcelain, chrome, and steel. As the light plays on these articles, glitter in the nicer sense of the word is added to the room.

The materials used for the accessories for informal backgrounds do

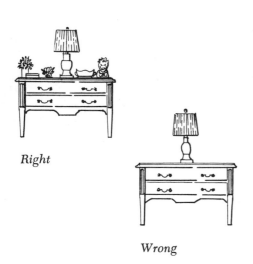

Right

Wrong

Formal

Informal

not have as much sparkle as those for a formal room with its crystal, gold leaf, and silver, but that is as it should be. Brass, bronze, pewter, copper, pottery and glass are informal and good no matter what the setting. Nevertheless, thought should be given to the choices in order to present an integrated whole. An overly elaborate crystal chandelier is as out of place in an Early American interior as sneakers are with an evening dress.

Objects of painted metal, called Toleware, can be delightful additions in either decor. Generally black, a universal color, they can be a smart touch with other colors. Toleware other than black is most captivating if it matches other colors in the room.

Only large objects should be placed on the mantel because no one enjoys looking at "pretties" they have to strain to see. Generally speaking, a symmetrical arrangement is best on the mantel because it automatically draws the eye to the center. For some reason, the

Wrong

Right

Formal Arrangement

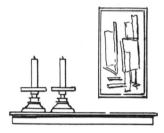

Informal Arrangement

average American housewife is always seeking a display that is different and unusual for this spot, although I feel no crying need for such individuality. Objects placed on it should be particularly lovely because the mantel is an attention-seeker. If the display constitutes the usual picture on the wall above and matching vases or candlesticks on each side, perhaps with a wide bouquet of flowers or clock in the middle, the decoration is adequate. Included as well can be sculpture, figurines and busts. In an informal interior such as Early American or Danish Modern, you may prefer to arrange your mantel asymmetrically. Such a grouping is much more difficult to do successfully, and it can become trying after a long stand, but it is cozier than a symmetrical arrangement.

Since a coffee table usually has a fairly large surface, correspondingly large accessories look good on it. But do not overcrowd it because it is the table that bears the brunt of any activity around the sofa. A poor bet for it is an item such as a high vase containing long-stemmed flowers which runs the risk of being knocked over or blocking a conversation across the table. Yet how often our top decorators are guilty of this misuse. Obviously, their rooms must be for display only.

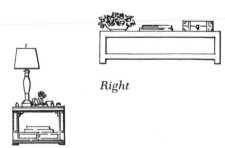

Right

End table accessories should be small because the lamp already takes up much of the room. Here is the place for little sentimental mementoes and other petite articles. A new accessory is a small tripod placed on skirted tables or end tables. Such a stand can be used to support an antique plate, a small print or an oil painting. The de-

Right

vice shows off items well in an unusual fashion. The number of objects to be so displayed is up to you, and may actually depend on how you feel about dusting. Remember, though, that one of the finest assets of a beautiful home is highly-polished wood on table tops and floors.

Right

A number of women are confused when it comes to choosing accessories. Their problem probably lies in the fact that they do not study detail well enough. You can avoid the problem by noticing the detail of beautiful rooms or by studying detail in magazine illustrations instead of always looking at the room as a whole. What type of room is it? What kind of accessories are displayed? Once you have these ideas firmly in your mind, you can make your own purchases with greater ease. Accessories give character to a room and can be almost anything within reason. Reason constitutes not using a human skull for a flower pot, as I saw in one home.

Wrong

An accessory should be something you love. It is not a necessity, as are draperies and a sofa. You really do not have to have it and you certainly do not have to buy all you need in one afternoon. There is so much visual pleasure in an accessory and so little function. Each is a pleasure to be enjoyed. So take your time purchasing them. After all, we would have nothing to anticipate if a home were decorated at one sweep.

Now that we know what articles make a home appear warm and friendly, let's find out how to put them together successfully. There is more to it than just buying things. I asked my husband what he thought made a livable home, and received a quick answer: "A good wife." So, you see, it is essentially up to you.

Principles of Art

The principles of art—harmony, balance, proportion, emphasis, and rhythm—naturally apply to home decoration. However, popular styles sometimes go against these principles. Like any small vice, such innovations can be refreshing and acceptable as long as they are not overdone. Yet they probably do not stay in style for too long. If you have adopted them, you must have a good sense of timing and replace them when they obviously have run their course. Here are a few used in this century that have gone by the board: crocheted antimacassars, plate rails, bureau runners, beaded lampshades, free form coffee tables, venetian blinds, unframed mirrors, and enormously tall table lamps. Whether it is good or bad, when a human being sees a style often enough he gets used to it, and in his eyes it becomes acceptable.

At times, a successful decorator can lay aside the best principles of art and still produce an extremely inviting idea. An example is a dark ceiling in the same room with a light floor. It was rather a bomb shell when a decorator introduced it twenty-five years ago because we were used to the opposite. Nature presents us with a dark earth and a light sky, and we liked the interior of our homes more or less to repeat the arrangement. It was unconsciously the natural way to do it. Yet we adjusted readily to the dark beamed ceilings with white rugs on the floor, finding the light floor a handsome foil for the bright colors used on our upholstered furniture. To innovate like the professional decorator is much more difficult for the amateur. Imagination is a wonderful thing, but when the average homemaker goes out on a limb in creating something for the house she must temper it with practicality and good taste.

A long time ago I entered a small bathroom that was completely lined with a shaggy, white cotton carpeting—floor, side walls, and ceiling. I had not known previously that I was prone to suffer from claustrophobia, but I did when I entered that tomb. The carpet fibers hanging down from the ceiling resembled a thousand small worms. The result was a feeling not conducive to comfort. Then I remembered that the household included three boys. We all know how boys wash. They run cold water over their hands, ignore the soap, and wipe the dirt off on the nearest towel. In the bathroom of the carpeted walls, if the boys missed the towel a bit the carpet served as a good substitute. Thus we have an example of an original idea being nothing but foolhardy.

Victorian—Wrong

Bad taste in art is not restricted to the individual. The Victorian period, for instance, produced almost nothing worth saving for posterity because the age had little feeling for good design or beauty in appearance; it emphasized bulky curves and angular embellishments. We, too, seem to be headed into a period of overdecoration, as indicated by the latest trends stressing wild clashes of color and design. I have recently seen in magazines such abortive items as lounge chairs that resemble piled-up inner tubes covered in an oversized herringbone pattern of shocking pink backed up to a wallpaper of blues and turquoise. If there is beauty in that, then I am as out of kilter with the modern tempo as "the surrey with the fringe on top."

Modern—Wrong

An item or two out of harmony with the other furnishings in a room may give it distinction and character; but when the major ideas clash, the result is confusion, tension and a constant impression of movement—all of which hardly lend themselves to the cultivation of livability. Remember that understanding the basic principles of art enables one to choose the best that is offered. Beauty and practicality are partners in creation. An idea is worthless if it cannot be applied.

Of the principles of art, harmony is the most important. We all know what harmony connotates, and we realize that without it the home would resemble a madhouse. What is it, however, in terms of home decorating? Harmony is a combination of parts that form a consistent and orderly whole. I believe most of us unconsciouly seek harmony for the background of our home.

We basically prefer horizontal and vertical lines and are at peace with them because they are in harmony with us and our background. On the other hand, the diagonal line is very much in the foreground in today's designing, but its introduction to a room should be uncomplicated and limited.

If we hold the diagonal line to the design in an area rug and perhaps tied-back draperies, the result merely causes a busy look, a voguish effect; it does not destroy the basic sense of harmony. But if large pieces of furniture placed on the diagonal, upholstery lively with diverse line movement, and pictures hung in stair formation on the wall are used along with them, the net result is confusion because there would be too much out of line with gravitation.

Fortunately, we are not limited to vertical and horizontal lines; another line comes into play a great deal in home decorations—the curved or transitional line. Soft and feminine, nature uses the curve constantly.

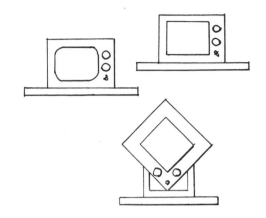

There are many ways in which we can relate harmony to interiors. We might, for instance, take a portable television set, retangular in shape. The picture repeats the lines of the outside box, so it is harmonious and easy to look at. Often, too, the picture area has rounded corners to break the severity of the straight lines. Here we see the use of the transitional line. Now, if the outside case were diamond in shape, made up of diagonal lines, the rectangular lines of the picture area inside would be annoying to the eye. The outside case would also be in conflict with the horizontal top of the chest on which it is placed and thus would be out of harmony.

We can show how harmony can be applied to draperies. Draperies generally hang straight and are thus in harmony with the lines of the window and the lines of the room. With the invention of the

traverse track, and the disappearance of the sheer curtain and window shade, out of necessity all draperies were hung straight. About ten years ago a change was introduced. We decided to ignore the traverse track, over single windows at least, and tie the draperies back. Pulled back in a severe diagonal manner, draperies add a harsh dominant line to a room. If there are too many single windows, the severe line may result in much confusion and too much attention and may not be worth the treatment. If, however, the drapery is pulled back softly in a curved transitional line, it is more pleasant in appearance, less disturbing, but still of course not as simple or as harmonious as it would be if the drapery hung straight. The fault lies in the fact that overelaborate drapery treatments often cause windows to become the chief center of interest in a room.

On a wide picture window, the result of tying back draperies is extremely dramatic. It always reminds me of a theater, and I am waiting for the curtain to drop and the show to end so I can go home. You need a dressy room to get away with this arrangement. If you feel the urge for tied-back draperies on a wide window, you do not necessarily have to arrange them to meet in the middle, but

only to come over the window around twenty-five inches on each side. Now there is a dynamic diagonal line that forces the eye to move upward. It ends suddenly at the introduction of the rod and is stranded there in space. The eye easily follows a diagonal line up, but works hard to follow it down. That is not true when draperies are hung straight; the eye can go up and down with ease and is not forced to jump to the horizontal line of the rod. Obviously, a valance then supplies the finishing touches to the tied-back drapery on the picture window. It would pull the two ends together as well as cover up the distracting rod. This valance can be as simple or as elaborate as you wish, but will be more finished in appearance sporting a fringe or binding. If you like the clean-cut, neat look, tied-back draperies are not for you, or for that matter any frilly drapery arrangement.

Diagonal lines show up in furniture designing every now and then. Surprisingly popular is the slanting leg. It arrived on the decorating scene in the informal, heavy, country furniture of the early Renaissance. The clever Europeans recognized its look of insecurity, and in order

Right

Wrong

to keep the table from appearing to have wanderlust they tied the legs together with a stretcher. No doubt they were also thinking of added strength. Shelved for centuries, the idea did not return to any extent until recently, and unfortunately often minus the stretcher.

Harmony must also be considered in room arrangement. Before decorating became an established profession in the United States, large pieces of furniture were often placed on the diagonal in a room, even to the extent that the bed and the chiffonier were placed across various corners. Such large pieces of furniture as chests and sofas are awkward and cause discord if they do not follow the lines of the room because the repetition of line movement is restful and fosters pleasant living. Conflicting lines of any magnitude in a room

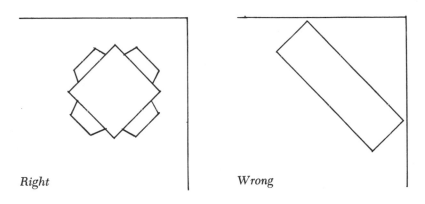

Right | *Wrong*

are inharmonious and make the room appear busier than a small boy trying to give the cat a bath. If the sofa is a cute little curved Victorian love seat, it is possible to set it in a corner because the curved line of the back cuts the diagonal to a gentle transitional. It would be even more appealing to place a large plant or lovely screen behind the love seat to soften the inharmonious line caused by the corner.

It follows then that today's tendency to go back to the discordant diagonal method of arranging a room with large pieces of furniture is discouraging. The only advantage I can see is that the lost corners offer great hiding places for the children with their occasional rainy day games of hide and seek. It makes sense to place either a writing desk or a game table across a corner because a corner allows extra space for a side chair. Today the desk has joined the togetherness fad, and instead of making its occupant look directly at a blank wall the chair placed along a wall allows the occupant to gaze into the room. Unless the desk is butted against a window, there is no doubt that the desk chair facing into the room is much more satisfying. The space available may alter the advisability of this arrangement, however, because the placement of the chair may force the desk to be too far out into the room. An otherwise wasted corner swallows up the desk chair without stealing valuable space.

The principle works the same way with the fourth chair at the game table. Here is a good example of going against the best principles of art but coming up with an idea so practical that it overrides the principle. If, however, we place a stereo cabinet across a corner, we discover the space behind the stereo is lost except as a dust catcher, and the cabinet itself cuts into two walls. The effect is awkward and unnecessary.

At times, a bay window is large enough to take a sofa. If we are aiming at harmony, then a straight sofa with rectangular end tables

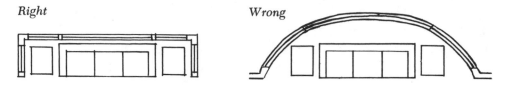

Right *Wrong*

could be placed in a rectangular bay, and a curved sofa with round end tables in a half-moon bay.

Not every piece of furniture in a room needs to conform to the lines of the room. If every piece of furniture is placed on the square, so to speak, the effect may be too formal and cold. Upholstered pieces, other than sofas or love seats, may be fittingly set on the

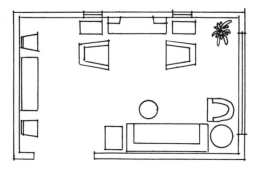

Formal—Right

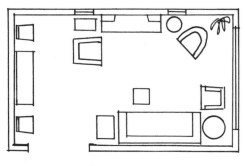

Informal—Right

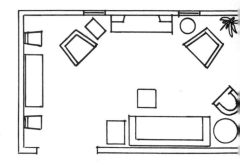

Informal—Wrong

diagonal to make a group around a sofa, table, or fireplace. If the room is large and every chair is situated in such a way, it again may cause more confusion than the patches on a beggar's coat, and a better situation would be reached if some were placed on the curve and some straight.

If you are planning to purchase a chair that is to take its place out from a corner, the best shape for the back of the chair is curved, not straight. Here again the transitional line is prettiest. As we near the center of the room, the straight lines of the wall recede in the background and the shape of the back of the chair placed on the diagonal becomes less and less prominent. You will discover that even the shape of a table next to a chair set in a corner should be scrutinized and that a round or an octagonal table takes its place there much more readily than a rectangular one. A rectangular table at this location just adds to the jumble of diverse, disturbing angles.

The placing of pictures on the wall often causes consternation for the housewife. Harmony can be achieved with pictures by hanging them on one level, instead of causing a climbing stairs impression on the wall. Many is the time I have seen the far wall in a dining ell sadly holding up two small staggered prints. The prints both are far too small for the wall and lead the eye up a diagonal path,

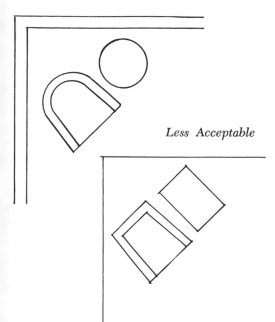

Acceptable

Less Acceptable

leaving it suspended in the middle of nowhere. The human eye is more at ease if it can ground itself, and these arrangements leave no way for the eye to rest. To repeat, the eye easily follows a diagonal line up, but it has difficulty following the same route down.

A good decorator might stagger pictures on the wall, but he so arranges them that the eye easily descends to furniture under the picture arrangement. Over a small chest, the eye would be able to follow the motion down because of some table object, such as a lamp, placed under the higher of the two paintings. Some women cannot hang two pictures level, but must always place one higher than the other. When this arrangement is carried throughout the house, it becomes tiring and in no way creates harmony. If a room is lacking in interest and motion, this idea might be executed with care in one or two places. It is best to remember to lead the eye up to something. On either side of a secretary, pictures could lead the eye up to it as the center of the group. Only on staircases does it truly make sense to continue this step effect since one is following the lines of the steps. Why, then, can't it be done logically when the opposite occurs? The long lines of the sofa are straight, and those are the lines to follow when hanging pictures—not, as sometimes occurs, a shed roofline above. The paintings hang closer to the sofa than to the ceiling.

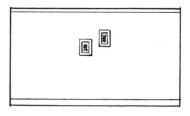

Wrong

Right

Wrong

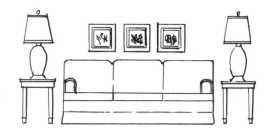

Right

There is also harmony between the size of a room and the amount of furniture used in it. A large room can be sparsely furnished and a small room overfurnished. A large room's good point is space, and it should not be made to look like an overcrowded hotel lobby by loading it with one sitting arrangement backed up to another. A small room creates a hemmed-in feeling, and the more that is placed in it—not, of course, beyond the bounds of common sense—the more enjoyable it becomes. Contemporary homes often have whole walls of glass that open the room to the outdoors. Such a construction increases

the feeling of space, and the styles of furniture that are most flattering to these rooms are the restrained periods such as Oriental or Danish Modern. Early American which we have translated to mean cute and cozy, is at its worst in a room with walls of glass. So look at the size of your room and the extent of your outdoor vistas, and decorate accordingly.

Within the room itself we should also be careful to combine furniture sizes harmoniously. If you own a huge, overstuffed modern sofa and place a delicate Louis XV occasional chair next to it, the effect is ridiculous. If, however, the occasional chair is moved across the room next to normally sized furniture, the result is not incongruous.

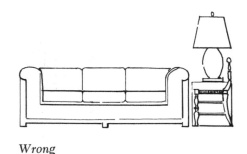

Wrong

Side chairs look out of place sitting next to sofas because they do not have enough body to take that location. But if they are low and squatty and are placed on the far side of the coffee table with intervening lounge chairs next to the sofa, the difference in weight is not so noticeable. Yet you would need two side chairs in this location. Much preferred would be open arm chairs, which are large enough to be in proportion. Side chairs are well named; they are best at the side of the room against a wall that makes their storklike appearance look proportionate. Side chairs generally have attractively decorated backs that show up much better when the plain wall surface works as a framework for the design.

There is also harmony in texture to consider, although most people do not have trouble along this line. It is obvious that silk satin does not go with burlap. On decorating a room, think of all its components and be sure that they are harmonious together. If they are, then the room is certain to be a pleasant one.

Acceptable

Proportion is the relationship that exists between things or parts of a thing and is involved to a great extent with size. The number of shapes in this world is limited. The ones we recognize most readily are the square, rectangle, circle, triangle and oval. Any complicated shape is the result of a combination of these basic forms. Some shapes give more pleasure to the eye than others. The most favored is the rectangle with its proportions of two to three. It is simple, yet has variation beyond the square and circle. The rectangle itself is found again and again within the home. Tables, pictures and rugs are usually this shape. The arch of the circle is the simplest and most monotonous form and actually has little in common with a vertical wall space. This is one of the reasons why there are so few round framed pictures except in miniature size. They are not as appealing esthetically as the rectangular form. Mirrors come in a greater variety of shapes than pictures. I would not purchase round or oval framed mirrors unless the frames were elaborate, almost Chippendale in style. A simple frame on a round mirror resembles a porthole piercing the wall rather than a proper decorative ornament. When I see one I feel like poking my head through it to see what is happening on the other side. You should avoid placing unrelated shapes on walls because vertical and horizontal lines show up strongly in this situation.

A great many people do not seem to realize that the reason pic-

Less Acceptable

tures are hung above pieces of furniture is that the average picture is out of proportion to the size of the wall on which it is placed. It begins to look lonely there. We therefore relate pictures to the size of the furniture underneath, and when one picture is too small we add more until the space is correctly proportioned. Sometimes, because of openings into rooms or because of a particular furniture arrangement, we find ourselves left with a large empty wall. It is far better to leave it empty than to place one tiny picture on it.

In order to achieve a correct look, a large wall space with no furniture placed against it needs a group of pictures or perhaps a huge abstract painting hanging on it. There are smaller wall spaces that do not need and some so small they cannot even take, a piece of furniture against them. In such cases one picture, or perhaps two, one above the other, suffices to allay that empty look. Do not feel that every wall space must have pictures. Sometimes it is a pleasant relief for the eye to gaze at empty places. Conversely, pictures always look well above large pieces of furniture. It is hard to feature a well-decorated home without some object of interest on the fireplace wall or over the sofa, the stereo or the buffet. Their placement cannot be judged the day you move in, but must be thoughtfully worked out.

When I have a group of pictures to hang, I first measure the wall space on the floor and fool around with the pictures until I hit upon the arrangement I like best. Then, using newspaper, I cut out the shape of each picture, and place the newspaper patterns on the wall with masking tape as they were laid out on the floor. Only after I live with it a few days to make sure I like the arrangement do I get out the hammer and nails. Tend to situate heaviness in the middle of the arrangement, and if there must be a difference in height the greatest height should be centered toward the imaginary center line.

For a while, decorators were hanging pictures so ridiculously low that the narrow margin left at the bottom was not in proportion to the other margins, so it is possible to hang pictures too low. But most of you could probably move your pictures ten inches lower and achieve a more lived-in look. Pictures should be in relationship to the furniture above which they are hung, and the eye should be able to take the whole group in at one glance and not have to jump from the piece of furniture to the picture arrangement. There are no exact measurements to make it easy for you. The test is to go across the room and look at your arrangement. If your eye must leap from one to the other, you are way off and the picture or pictures must be lowered.

One piece of furniture should have only one group of pictures above it; thus, our spacing between pictures also becomes important. Hanging one painting on one side of the sofa and another on the other side is incorrect. It leaves a void in the middle. The space between the objects hung on a wall should be smaller than the objects themselves considered as a group.

Another good point to remember when you are arranging groups of objects on the wall is that the objects should not take up the full

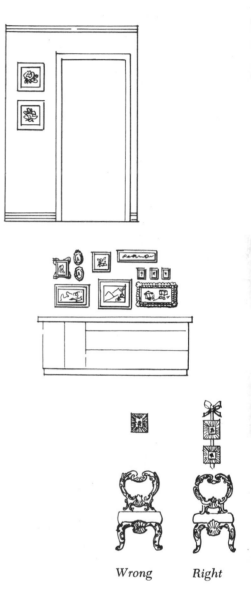

Wrong   *Right*

Wrong

Wrong

width of the piece of furniture underneath but should leave a border, so to speak. Neither should they extend beyond the furniture that is the base of the group. In our world, heaviness tends to stay close to the earth and substance becomes lighter and lighter as it ascends. It is reversed for the group on the wall to be wider than the furniture underneath. The arrangement causes a feeling of unrest. A child learns this premise early in life with his building blocks. When the top outweighs the bottom, the whole structure usually comes tumbling down.

In the hallways of houses built during the past twenty years we generally place a small chest. On the wall above it should go a high vertical shape such as a mirror or a painting or a group of small pictures. The reason for the choice of the long vertical object is obvious. It needs to hang at standing eye level, but the space between the piece of furniture and the wall object must not be so great as to separate their dependence.

Many women are dubious about relieving the monotony of the back hall. Generally, unless it is wider than average, I would not worry too much about it. It is fundamentally a passage and there is no particular reason to make it an attention seeker. A pretty wallpaper of a block, medallion, or quiet flowing flower design can take away its bareness. If you desire pictures, they do not need to be placed in groups, but situated one after the other with a good space in between as a picture gallery might present them. Family photographs often go here, and although it is an excellent place for them it is becoming somewhat old hat by now. Whatever the subject matter, though, the pictures should be hung at a standing eye level.

Odd numbers are more appealing than even numbers. Seven and eleven have been the lucky ones in gambling throughout history, and in English they even rhyme. The number three has a particular magical quality to us and even shows up in religion (Father, Son and Holy Ghost), in politics (liberty, fraternity, equality), and in design (the trefoil, or fleur-de-lis, which has been a popular motif through the ages). So three is indeed a number for you to remember when you are arranging items on your table or chests. On one side of your large coffee table three accessories used together, such as an ash tray, cigarette box and lighter, would be more effective than just an ash tray and cigarette box. Three pictures above a stereo would be better than two. In furniture arrangement, a sofa flanked by a chair on either side, making a group of three, is more flattering than just one chair on one side. In a dining room, a buffet looks far better with a dining chair at each side than just one at one side.

Another reason for aiming at this sort of balance, of course, is that the eye may be carried effectively inward toward the center of interest. Even numbers tend to be monotonous and do not offer enough diversity to delight the eye. The number three offers variety yet does not disturb the balance. Even so, if one is not careful in arranging, odd numbers can also be dull. For instance, the symmetrical placement of objects for a mantel arrangement could be dull if the

Acceptable

Less Acceptable

Wrong   *Right*

picture on the wall and the candlesticks on each side were exactly the same height and if the spacing from the end of the mantel to the candlestick and from the candlestick to the picture were equal. But if the picture were hung higher and the candlesticks were placed nearer to the edge of the mantel, the spacing would create interest in the group.

After World War II when architects planned the fireplace off-center in the so-called ranch house, they usually found a need to extend the brick and the mantel all the way to the corner. The extended mantel somehow found its way to the drawing board from our Early American kitchens. It is punishment enough to stand the fireplace near a corner, let alone force it to wear the dunce hat of an elongated shelf. The device created a display area more than double the usual shelf length, and as a result it has been the despair of many housewives who have found it difficult to arrange attractively. Probably the best way to attack it would be to continue to treat the fireplace opening

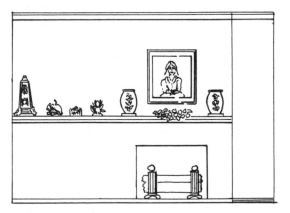

as the center of interest, placing a good-sized painting or print directly above it. Tall vases, for instance, could be placed on each side of this center location. The accessories to be arranged on the section of the mantel extending to the wall would then be high on the fireplace opening, declining in height in the middle and rising to a greater height again in the corner. Objects can be placed either singly or in groups.

Floors also come into this discussion. The curved leg of Louis XV furniture looks best on rugs having floral patterns. The French designed their Aubusson and Savonnerie rugs well supplied with curved lines. As the furniture leg changed to straight and tapered, the rug pattern became more severe in order to match. The oriental rugs that marry best with our modern straight furniture are those designs filled with stiff geometric forms rather than with natural flowing ones. Architects with their educated tastes and preference for modern architecture find these gay but stylized orientals distinguished backdrops for their homes.

A round area rug is visibly in accord with a round dining room table. Area rugs can present problems with the dining table. They must be large enough to allow all the chairs to push out without going over the edge of the rug when one is trying to sit down. A lovely dinner party can come to a complete halt as the guests try to extract their chairs from the curled up rug edge. Because our dining rooms are now so small, we may find that after we have installed a rug large enough to take care of the problem we no longer have merely an area rug. Here, then, we can either repeat the line of the table and use a round rug or use a square or rectangular rug. An ideal room-sized rug leaves twelve inches between it and the wall. Under dining room tables, rugs are usually more practical than wall-to-wall carpeting. The designs in them tend to camouflage stains. Since the dining room is a somewhat cold room with so much wood surface showing, a pretty patterned rug gives it the warmth and variety it needs.

Horizontally dividing a wall surface into two or more sections has always been popular. Lower ceilings create less demand for division, but we are going back to this construction even though our floor-to-rafter space is usually a skimpy eight feet. A wall may be marked for division at the halfway point, as it is indeed in some bathrooms where the tile stops and the plaster begins. This is a dull division, somehow much too even to appeal to the eye. Don't try it yourselves with wood paneling and plaster in that new room you are adding to the back of your home. I have seen this tasteless spectacle too often. Consider instead the ratio of one-third panelling to two-thirds plaster.

Wrong

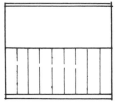

We can copy the Victorians and go back to the dropped ceiling, which involves a picture molding around the room approximately twenty-four inches down from the ceiling. Instead of putting nails into the walls to hold up pictures, the Victorians carried a picture wire up into an S hook that connected to the molding. The space between the picture molding and the ceiling matched the ceiling rather than the side wall. This arrangement has a visual advantage in a room with high ceilings, but it is overpowering with our eight-foot ceilings.

Following that fashion, the plate rail became popular in dining rooms from the turn of the century until the depression years, even though room height was lowered. All the housewives' little goodies were distributed on this narrow shelf, way above eye level, touched only to be washed during the spring cleaning and mostly forgotten for the rest of the year. As a style, it was out of kilter with the best principles of art because it attracted attention to items, often much too small, far above eye level, causing frustration. Objects worthy to be seen should be placed in a room in such a way that they can be enjoyed.

If we must have knickknacks displayed on high shelves, let us at least continue with more shelves underneath until we approach a piece of furniture. In this way, at least, the eye is carried pleasantly to the topmost shelf and down again. Too often we leave hanging shelves, pregnant with overload, suspended midwall with no support

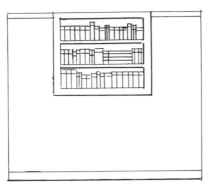

Wrong

Right

from a piece of furniture underneath. Please give shelves the support they need with a chest, desk or long table.

It is difficult to hang shelves over upholstered furniture. When you place a shelf high enough to keep heads from colliding with it (an absolute necessity if you wish to keep friends), then the space between it and the chair or sofa is so great that the group seems awkward. Today, large shelves for books are generally built from the floor to the ceiling or at least up from the floor to a logical stopping place.

Kitchens, too, are catching this high perch disease. Kitchens have long been removed from the clinical look of the 1930's. Our fore-bears hung everything on the walls and from the ceilings for lack of cupboards. If you go in for this quaint style, the hanging objects should be those used by the housewife, and not just there for display.

When our kitchen cupboards do not reach the ceiling, we find it difficult not to make use of the broad shelf created at the top of the cupboards, and sooner or later it becomes jammed with articles, including (I hope the kitchen stool and watering can are handy) plants. Although crowding this shelf may make a kitchen seem cozy, it is a troublesome display area. Objects placed on the shelf should be large so they can be seen easily from the room, they should be arranged interestingly, and they should be kept clean and shining.

Long ago, chateaux, villas and manor houses had tremendously high ceilings, as well as horizontal moldings that extended down from the ceiling and up from the floor. That molding was often called a chair rail because it was about the height of the top of a side chair. Even today it is artistically the most attractive way to divide a wall horizontally because it is not monotonous as is a half-

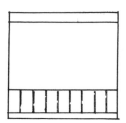

and-half division and because it is not out of eye level as is the picture molding. It is also practical in dining rooms: chair backs hit the molding and thus do not scar the plaster or wallpaper. This trim, popular in old Williamsburg, is making inroads today as eighteenth-century furniture experiences a revival. Your husband can purchase moldings at the local lumber yard. Along with them, you need a baseboard and cornice with trims around doors and windows. The end result can add immeasurably to the worth of your house.

Valances are often out of proportion in depth to the height of a room. This error easily occurs in a room with an eight-foot ceiling when the housewife wishes to hide the drapery rod as well as exhibit a more elaborate window treatment. Actually, a valance of only about twelve inches deep is correct. When it is extended from the window top to the ceiling, it becomes ludicrous. There is nothing wrong with showing wall space between the valance top and the ceiling. You may not need it, though, if your ceiling is high enough and if the window rises in height accordingly. With a ten-foot ceiling, a window could easily crown itself with a fifteen- to eighteen-inch cornice that would elegantly extend from it to the ceiling.

One of the most ridiculous drapery treatments to be seen is the one that terminates at the ceiling and cuts itself off short four inches below the sill. The function of the drapery is to cover the window area. It has been the fashion in all but the most cottage-type of interiors to drop the drapery to the floor rather than to end it just below the sill. This arrangement pleases the eye. The only reason to take the drapery up to the ceiling would be to create a feeling of height, which is utterly destroyed when the drapery ends at the

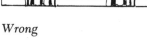

Wrong

Wrong

Right

apron. Yet the most flagrant mistake of all is to end the drapery midway between the apron and the floor.

We often like draperies to reach from wall to wall and from floor to ceiling to give an expansive feeling. If, with an average height ceiling, a valance is added at the ceiling, wall space is in evidence from the top of the window to the bottom of the valance (if the correct proportions are followed) so that often a sheer curtain should be added; in any case, be sure that the wall is the same color as the draperies. You can see the result if the wall is painted forest green and the draperies are white. A much too heavy rectangle of color is exhibited above all the windows in a room. It is more sensible to start

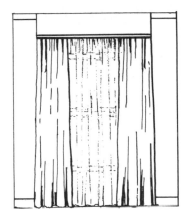

Wrong   *Right*

your draperies about four inches from the window top and to carry them to the floor in the main areas of the house. Follow this instruction especially in a room having windows of different sizes. If you have to carry the draperies to the floor in the living room because the glass goes all the way to the floor, the draperies over the normal silled window in the dining room should be similarly treated. It is bad enough for all these unmatching architectural openings to exist in contemporary homes without ending the draperies at different lengths.

A window over a bed, so wide yet so short, finds itself perched high on the wall like a spread eagle surveying the master bedroom. As unattractive as it is, we must live with it in order to find a place for all our furniture in such bedrooms and still have a cross draft. Think of what happens architecturally in these rooms. We have a whole wall of closets, a door coming into the room, another one going to the master bathroom, and even a wall of glass with a sliding door leading to the patio. The furniture, including a triple dresser and a king-size bed, is up against it, so the high window becomes really necessary. The only position for the bed is under it.

Since this window, above eye level, is awkwardly shaped, it is best to treat it as simply as possible. It may be handled architecturally, rather than decoratively, by filling the space with shutters (painted to match the wall), or perhaps by something like a shoji screen. Because the window is so different from an ordinary one, you would not have to duplicate the shutters in any other window in the room. But any fabric used should be repeated in the other draperies. Under these circumstances, the color of the fabric should match the color of the wall. This decree unfortunately eliminates the use of unusual fabric for the bedroom draperies. You would not want a wild cabbage rose chintz covering an area this high on the wall.

If such uniformity bores you to death, you could use a lively print, wall-to-wall and floor-to-ceiling, on the bed wall, making a vivid backdrop for the bed. This arrangement might call for a sheer curtain, also wall-to-wall and floor-to-ceiling, to hang across the the opening, or at least a simple sheer pulled taut on the window glass. The bed-

spread could match or be without design, emphasizing one of the colors in the fabric of the draperies. You might even have a valance over the whole plan. The draperies could tie back to give a regal effect, especially with straight sheers going to the floor behind and a window shade on the glass. At any rate, once this wall becomes loaded with fabric, the drapery treatment would be minimized on the other windows in the room. Even with a sliding glass door, I would hang the draperies just over the opening. To go wall-to-wall and floor-to-ceiling for the second time in one room would be overwhelming yet incomplete. You might as well finish the job by synchronizing all the walls with fabric until it resembles an Arab's tent.

Another problem that arises is the placement of long furniture in a long and narrow room. A long sofa should be placed along the long wall, with smaller pieces, acting like camouflage, filling the short wall. If the sofa is placed along the short wall, it announces to one and all the awkward dimensions of the room.

Before we leave proportion, we should mention a badly designed piece of furniture that floods the market—the high back dining chair. It is a throw back to the Italian Renaissance when high back chairs were in perfect proportion to the high ceilings, and they were saved

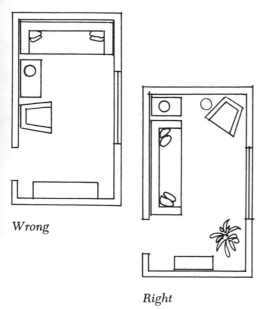

Wrong

Right

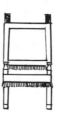

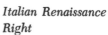

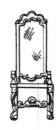

Italian Renaissance
Right

English Jacobean
Wrong

in design by being broad of beam as well. Since modern high-backs are copied from the English Jacobean style, they are skinny. Six of these creatures lined up at a dining room table look as if you had invited a herd of giraffes for dinner. Besides, they are rarely comfortable to sit in. Unless designed with a fiddle back, they hit the shoulder blades in the wrong location. Perhaps the most uncomfortable chair ever designed is the rush-seated, high ladder-back chair. The rungs manage to hit the back in all the wrong places all the way up.

Balance, the third principle of art, is a state of equilibrium. It works like a seesaw and is easy to understand. Equal weights are balanced when they are equal distances from the center. When the weights are unequal the heavier of the two must be moved closer to the imaginery center line to achieve steadiness. So whenever you arrange furniture, objects on top of chests, or pictures on walls, you should remember the simple principle of the seesaw. Decorators who lack formal training often commit this *faux pas*. It is an extremely helpful rule since, for instance, one can use both a lamp and a large ash tray on a long console table and yet balance the arrangement. The lamp would be placed nearer to the imaginery center line and the ash tray farther away from it. Now that you know this easy rule, you can notice how often articles are unknowingly arranged in just the opposite manner. In any event, it is best to avoid placing too much weight on one side.

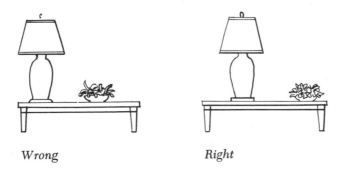

Wrong   *Right*

Human beings like balance and unconsciously become upset when a room's furnishings are arranged like those of a ship at sea during a bad storm.

There are two kinds of balance in decorating, formal and informal. Formal, or symmetrical balance, occurs when objects that are equally alike in their ability to attract attention are used at an equal distance from the imaginery center line. Formal balance has been popular in the western world all through history. In decorating, it is more restful and easier to organize than informal balance. It can produce a cold impression and if used consistently throughout a room would make it seem out of touch with the friendly atmosphere we wish to achieve.

Informal balance is generally preferred in the United States these days. This asymmetrical balance, or disproportionate arrangement of furnishings, is obtained when articles different in their ability to attract attention are used together in a group. The less dressy a home

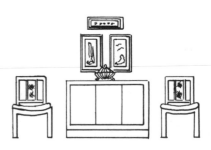

Formal

Informal

is and the busier the activities of the family are, the more appealing makes the room look lived-in. If you know of a room that exudes this type of balance becomes. It has an intimate quality about it that friendliness, an analysis might well uncover that the fact depends on a lack of symmetry. Correct asymmetry, or informality, is difficult to achieve because, even though articles in corresponding places do not match, there must be an allover balance so that the room is not out of kilter.

Furniture should be fairly well distributed throughout the room. Look at your living room and draw an imaginary line down the middle, first one way and then the other. If your pieces come close to matching in weight on each side of the line, then you have done a good job with balance. A dozen red roses to the lady who has! The living room found in the popular one-story house is likely to be too long and too narrow. This wind tunnel can present problems. There may also be a huge glass area on only one side of the room. The fireplace is probably placed off center. There may actually be no decent wall against which to arrange an eight-foot-long sofa plus end tables. It would seem that many architects are ignorant of furniture arrangement and of the types and sizes of furniture used in contemporary homes.

Strangely enough, an architectural opening such as an archway has more weight than a plain wall. For that reason the buffet in the dining room often looks best opposite the opening into the room, and a fireplace seems right when situated at the far side of the living room entrance.

Window walls also enter this weight problem. Too loud a fabric or too elaborate a style of drapery on a window wall can easily offset a room. At night there is no need to emphasize this opening because its function has shut down until daylight. On the other hand, single windows evenly distributed on more than one wall tell a different story. Here a window with a pretentious drapery treatment is at least normal in relationship to the walls of the room, and when repeated enough times they balance each other. In size, they are less eye catching than a normal sofa.

When you are arranging a room, the large pieces should be put in position first, then the more movable pieces, making groups around the larger ones. If an underlying balance has not been achieved, by finishing up with the accessories—lamps, pictures, decorator's pillows, and so forth—you can probably work out a perfect balance.

If your furniture can't be balanced, as in the case of a large wing chair on one side of the sofa and a lightweight occasional chair on the other, remember that color can be used for balance as well as weight. Perhaps the end tables and lamps do not match, either. The larger end table and the fatter lamp naturally would be more sensible next to the more comfortable wing chair, the preferred seating place of the two chairs, so the end result is definitely off balance. If, however, the occasional chair sports a bright color in comparison with the fabric on the wing chair, and if the small sofa pillows are only placed at the side near the occasional chair, good informal balance has been achieved.

How well that was understood a few years ago when connected sectionals and nine-foot-long sofas were the rule! The large sofas were often quietly upholstered in white or in beige, but the lounge chairs distributed around the room were brilliant in color like a peacock strutting before its mate. These colors were also repeated on the sofa pillows. In order to tie the whole room together, it was necessary to balance the color by repeating it in small amounts on the sofa, but it would have been much too much to have had the whole sofa done in a brilliant color or a loud print. If a huge sectional sofa were upholstered in brilliant purple, what could be done to make the smaller chairs weigh as much? However, as the seven- and six-foot sofas came to be preferred, we went further away from the light, soft colors and the print became appropriate again. Now that this large piece was finally trimmed down to size, the room could stand more vivid, busy covering. At last, housewives throughout the United States discovered what those who lived in the older traditional areas knew right along—that a heavy woven pattern is the most practical covering for a sofa.

It is interesting to see how one change in style can create such a conglomeration of problems that the outgrowth is a whole new chain of concepts. As the long sofa came into vogue, the coffee table grew like the national debt until suddenly the two pieces of furniture together made a lopsided room. It was discovered that balance could be reinstated if the coffee table, either round or rectangular, were moved across the room to rest by the esteemed picture window. There it acquired a tall lamp flanked by two chairs. Out of this arrangement was born the square coffee table, taking up so much less space but too diminutive for the social life that surrounds the sofa. On that small table top a tray balances precariously and the evening paper droops over its side. A solution of some sort had to evolve. Thus larger and more varied end tables came into existence, even to the point that the lady's writing desk was placed at the sofa's side. So remember, if you have gone in for a very small coffee table, make sure your end tables are large enough to permit anyone using the sofa to have space to put down a coffee cup, a magazine, knitting, or whatever he or she may be holding.

Furniture should be grouped according to its function, so it does seem queer, except in the smallest of homes, to have a desk butted up against a sofa. The quiet activities pursued at a desk have little in common with the home's social center. Although there is nothing wrong with placing a desk in a living room, it is somewhat shortsighted to join it with the conversation group. For the same reason, we would not place good lounging chairs on both sides of an upright piano. If chairs are so placed, they should be light enough to be carried across the room for party purposes.

A vast number of people today prefer to hang pictures in an informal manner. I wonder why it is that we are afraid of rigidity and feel that asymmetry is more flexible and less demanding? Strict adherence to a law seems stifling to our new concept of freedom no matter what facet of life involves us. Nothing is wrong with informality as long as the rest of the plan is thoughtfully worked out. The shape of the painting now becomes of concern. A rectangular painting, wider than it is high, asks to be centered above a piece of furniture. It looks cum-

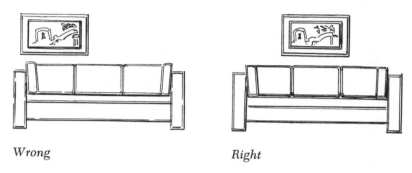

Wrong   *Right*

bersome off center. A painting that is high and narrow looks skimpy when placed by itself above the middle of a sofa; but if it is situated near one side in conjunction with a lamp on an end table, it does not look so woebegone anymore. The amount of furniture on the other

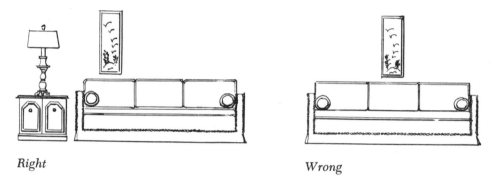

Right   *Wrong*

side of the sofa should generally be more than that used on the side with the painting. Extremely wide pictures may look better off center too, and the underlying balance would be treated the same way as the high, narrow frame. One might wish to arrange a group of small pictures off center, although this generally gives a ticky-tacky impression. They generally look best centered, remembering of course that the space covered by them must be in relation to the size of the sofa. Just keep adding more until the right dimensions of the wall are filled.

The off center arrangement with pictures is somewhat easier to attain correctly over a small chest or table. The balance manifests itself when a lamp, vase of flowers, statue, or any item large enough is placed on the opposite side. Small paintings placed one above the other, yet off center, are appealing to the eye in this case, probably because the individual pictures themselves do not seem too small for the size of the chest. But we must not forget the group as a whole. If upholstered furniture is on just one side of a chest or table, as well as a floor lamp, a picture arranged off center without any large object placed on the other side of the chest to counterbalance it would be all that is necessary because the chair and floor lamp would do the trick. Don't forget that the complete group should be taken into consideration

when one is concerned with balance. You can see that, in addition to all her other abilities, the homemaker must be one of the great jugglers in the world to balance a room full of furniture.

If wallpaper is placed on one wall only in a room, balance comes into play. The wall that is chosen for this honor must be an important center of interest, such as a bed wall in the bedroom or the buffet wall in the dining room. It would be incorrect to paper only one wall in a hall unless it were the front door wall in a wide hall. When wallpaper is used on only one wall, the other three walls must be painted to match the background of the paper. If the three walls are matched to the design instead, the background of the paper assumes an importance that is out of bounds and the wall recedes from view. Remember that nothing can overcome the weight problem if wallpaper is used on just two walls of a room. Actually, nothing is nicer than seeing an attractive paper on all four walls.

Emphasis is the principle that attracts the eye first to the most prominent item in an arrangement. One way we achieve emphasis is through the grouping of objects so that the eye follows a logical path to the center of interest. A living room is set up with various groups of furniture, and the eye should be brought into the center of each group to pause, so to speak, before going on to the next. If the separate sections are not defined, and emphasis not achieved, the room appears as mishmash. Along with arranging articles correctly, we attract attention by the use of decorations, by contrasting various colors, and by exposing designs to plain surfaces.

Emphasis is not difficult to achieve. The problem today is overemphasis. In our desire for change and individuality we are piling design upon design, clashing one loud color against another, until the eye does not know where to turn next. This motley, when carried to extremes, adds up to no emphasis at all. A successful room has a greater proportion of empty spaces than areas of emphasis. Rooms in which one spends a great deal of time should not have too dramatic a scheme or they can become tiresome. Entrance halls and bathrooms, for instance, can be of more lively decor than living rooms and bedrooms.

When you enter a room you should first be aware of the accessories and objets d'art, next of the furniture, then of the wall treatment, and last of all the floor. The area rug can be so obtrusive that it is not only the first item you notice in the room but also the most remembered when you leave. Whatever is covering the floor should stay down there. If you have a lively rug, you must use its color scheme as the basis for the room proper. Then, no longer incongruous with the general scheme, it takes its rightful place and emphasis on the floor. Even wall-to-wall carpeting is overemphasized if it it too striking a color instead of neutral. For instance, if olive green is your carpet preference, the color should not die on the floor, but persist elsewhere, perhaps on the sofa or on a pair of wing chairs. To ignore the carpet invariably suggests that you just moved in and had nothing to match the carpet you found there. Background colors, however, such as white, beige, gray, or cinnamon brown need not be repeated in the room. Their neutrality excludes them from taking part in the battle to be noticed.

On the other hand, a paralyzing red carpet demands that red be introduced if only on the sofa pillows and drapery trim.

Each room should have a center of interest. In the living room it is obviously the fireplace, an essential part of our ancient past. Thus, be sure that your most distinguished curios and other such objects are used to decorate the mantle and wall behind. Don't forget, your fireplace equipment is in focus, too, so they, too, should be good looking.

The sofa is the second most important center of interest in the living room, and if the home does not have a fireplace it becomes the most important. As I have stated, people gravitate to the sofa when they enter a living room, and as they walk toward it their eyes take in the detail surrounding it. As a result, your best-looking lamps should be here along with good-looking paintings; your most interesting accessories should be located on the end tables and the coffee table. Naturally, when your guests sit down, the coffee table is in full view; it should be attractively arranged. If people do not prefer to sit on your sofa after they have entered the living room, there is some reason for it. Perhaps your sofa is in an awkward location or the coffee table is too long and blocks the entrance.

Every now and then a living room in an older house has a dull, dark corner or two. Some housewives think that these areas need brightening up and often hang an especially loud painting in them. The result is that too much attention is drawn to a section that does not warrant it.

In the dining room, either the table or the buffet is the center of interest. Sofas change their coverings a few times throughout one's married life, or are even relocated to another room, but the dining room table is likely to stay put, staying with us to our graves. So buy a substantial one that is not too unusual in design, one that will last through various changes of decor.

Less Acceptable

All rooms have their big pieces: the dining room has the table; the bedroom, the bed; the library, the desk; the living room, the sofa. The furniture should be placed according to its use and the eye should be able to run pleasantly from one group to the other.

Acceptable

Often arising is the question of how to hang one large painting with two smaller ones in a symmetrical manner. In a formal arrangement, the large picture would naturally be centered and the two smaller ones arranged on each side. The two smaller paintings could line up with the large one at the top or at the bottom, or could be centered horizontally with the large one. The first arrangement, matching at the top, would be the least attractive because we do not enjoy heaviness above with emptiness in between. Lining them all up at the bottom to match the large frame would be fine, but perhaps best of all would be to have the horizontal center line of all the pictures match. This arrangement would emphasize the large center picture most, carrying the eye easily to the main attraction of this group of furniture and accessories.

Right

Notice the direction of the action or the placement of dominating color in your pictures. If you locate a painting off center and the subject is, let us say, galloping horses, the horses should gallop toward the middle of the sofa, not go off in the other direction. Any violent action or color should lead the eye inward, not outward. Even when you are

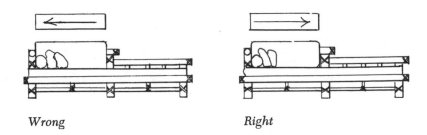

Wrong   *Right*

placing a group of paintings together, this principle should be taken into consideration. No one would think of placing two profiles back to back. Any other motion should be considered in the same way.

Rhythm, the least obvious art principle as far as interior decorating is concerned, is movement marked by the regulated succession of strong and weak elements. We do not deliberately seek rhythm in decorating a home. In fact, we may be more negative than positive in our approach to this factor.

The more pattern, the more rhythm, and too many patterns used together can cause confusion and restlessness. At the present time, patterns are back in favor. When they do not match in a room (more and more they do not), they must be handled with care, using quiet spaces in between; or you might also consider introducing sister prints. Otherwise desirable emphasis is lost. A room is full of unhappy sensations when the movement of the eye is kept fluttering. Yet in the latest method of mixing patterns, prints of all colors are splashed together everywhere in a room; the only obvious continuity is that they are small, allover patterns. Such a room has a 1910, predecorator-period quality about it and is, for lack of a better description, quaintly confusing.

Choosing a wallpaper must be done with great care, particularly if it is to be hung on all four walls. You must remember that what may appear charming in a small piece may be horrible when placed all over. Try to bring wallpaper-sample books home, see the pattern in the location in which you plan to use it, and do your best to visualize it all around the room.

Let us not forget that the diagonal line is the most restless line of all, and that when duplicated in a wallpaper it may be annoying in a room that is to be used frequently. Yet a herringbone pattern in a hall can be dramatic, a lattice pattern can be flattering for an outdoor effect in a dining nook, and a diamond design can be captivating in a bedroom that already lacks the vertical wall line, as happens with the sloping ceiling in a Cape Cod house. In the latter case, a block paper would be all wrong because the diagonal ceiling line would keep breaking into the vertical and horizontal silhouette.

Conspicuous diagonal lines are often found in area rugs today and, since they dominate, the design lends itself to the small rug far better than to room-size or wall-to-wall carpeting. Its Tom Thumb dimensions allow enough breathing space before the lines of the walls of the room are in evidence.

Rhythm must also be considered in the selection of furniture. We generally select pieces for their stability rather than for their movement, so we purchase pieces that exhibit straight lines for strength and restrained curves for gracefulness. No one wants a chair full of exaggerated curves. Furniture can also be too straight or severe in design.

Rhythm can be achieved by visually overlapping the placement of your accessories; don't separate them into their own little group. For example, if a round tray rests on a table against a wall, an added bouquet of flowers is more effective if nestled against the tray than if placed all by itself. Remember again that your home is not a picture gallery and that it produces a pleasant appearance to have the top of a bouquet extend over the frame into a picture. Any object on a mantel, chest or table can overlap a painting on the wall. It does not interfere with a picture that is merely another accessory. I would not go so far as to hang a picture directly behind a lampshade, but almost.

Now that we have combined the different elements of your room following the best of artistic principles, let's go on to color.

Wrong

Right

❧ 4

Color

Nothing contributes more to the beauty of our world than color. It consistently surrounds us. Think for instance of the silvery green quality of aspen leaves as the wind makes them dance in the sunlight. Now imagine a dull gray landscape, completely colorless: if you were surrounded by nothing else, what a drab existence you would have!

Color has a strong impact upon the decorations in a home. You could own the most expensive furniture and fabrics and have your living room perfectly arranged, but if your color scheme were poorly chosen it would take quite a while before your guests would notice the room's good qualities. If you had a beautiful color scheme, however, no matter what the style or the arrangement of the furniture, people would exclaim at once about the beauty of the room. Too many people are overly concerned with practicality and are afraid of growing tired of a definite color.

Light is color's master. Think of how much more color there is on a sunny day than on a cloudy one. The color is there; it is the light that is missing. Color actually changes from morning to night and from season to season. Inside the home the efficiency of color combinations depends on where they occur in a room, what is placed with them, and how much color is used. Simply make sure that the colors do not fight each other, and the result will probably be lovely.

Most people recognize a good color scheme when they see one. The problem appears to be a common inability to diagnose poor ones. Some people are born with a better color sense than others, just as some lucky people have a keen ear for music and others do not. Of course, a certain percentage of our population suffers from color blindness. Others see most colors as grays. I had two redheads in an interior decorating class a few years ago. One came to class in breathtaking colors that more than offset her gorgeous flaming red hair. The other, with equally lovely hair, did not appear to be considering her natural endowment in choice of clothes. Through a test I gave on color, I discovered that the second lady was unable to describe colors correctly; she was partially color blind. Unfortunately, she was much put out and refused to accept it when this was brought to her attention. It was too bad because with proper help she could have been as stunning as the other lady.

Arriving at beautiful color schemes is not too difficult if you put a little effort into it.

The greatest teacher of color is nature. So let us consider a color chart, which is man-made but modeled on the rainbow. Here we see what is called the law of the order of strength. Yellow, nature's lightest color, is placed at the top, and violet, her darkest, at the bottom, with the cool colors on one side and the warm colors on the other, both sides becoming darker in strength as they descend toward violet. When this order of strength is reversed, we have what we call discord. If you place light yellow next to dark violet, the result is acceptable and pleasant; but make the yellow a deep, deep mustard and the violet the lightest of lavenders, and one color looks dirty while the other appears insubstantial. There is no doubt about it, mustard and pale lavender together make about the ugliest color scheme conceivable. I have seen a bedroom with mustard walls and matching carpet, but a king-size bed sporting a light lavender bedspread. The result was upsetting. I also saw the combination used in a beauty parlor. There, a deep mustard wall alternated with a pale lavender one, and the result was ghastly. What a mistake for a *beauty* parlor to make!

Discord shows up most when the colors combined that come from opposite ends of the chart, but it can occur with colors much nearer to each other. Deep red and light gold can be rich and lovely together, but pale pink and mustard can be just awful. But you may not immediately see what is wrong. I was once asked to give my diagnosis of the cause of a displeasing cast in a teenager's bedroom. Recently painted by the girl herself in pale lavender, the whole room seemed harsh and unpleasant. It was a studio bedroom, and both the bed and boudoir chair were covered with a particularly strong royal blue fabric. The blue was just too much for the pale walls. By using a new bedspread of pale blue and a pretty white-background printed cover of purple, lavender and pale blue for the chair. I made the room livable again.

Obviously, we can set up rules to govern our selection of colors. Deep gold is at its best when used with deep green, orange, blue, or red. When deciding on pale lavender, keep the reds, blues, or whatever even lighter. These directions are particularly valid when using those colors in large amounts. If you study the best from the past in either Oriental or European works of art, you discover that this fundamental rule is followed to an amazing extent. As an example, in the handsome Moorish palace "Alhambra" in Granada, Spain, medium blues are much in evidence in the tiled walls. Yellow is the secondary color, but it is always the same hue or even lighter than the blue. The result is untiringly pleasing.

We need not get too involved in color schemes for the home. The simplest is the monotone scheme, which can produce a beautiful but not easily attained effect, because the use of one color can also create monotony. You would need to select with the greatest of care interesting accessories for the room because what has actually been created is a background in which these articles stand out keenly. Extreme modernists often choose this technique to make their abstract paintings the important items in the room. If you like to give parties and know many interesting people, this may be the color scheme for your living room because it sets the people off so brilliantly. Another caution to keep in mind when using this color scheme is the need for variety in texture. And interesting textures, like good-looking accessories, cost money. You can see how dull it would be if the floor were covered with a cut velvet carpet and the furniture upholstered in a velvet material all of the same hue. It would be difficult at a glance to tell where the carpet left off and the sofa began.

We think of monotone color schemes as mostly light in color, but a room can be done effectively in just one deeper color, such as red. You would want to use a range of red, perhaps even from pale pink to maroon, and you would want to include a great deal of white. Not a color in the true sense of the word, white can be a tremendous help in assuaging intensity.

Simple harmony is another color scheme. Harmonious colors are found next to each other on the color chart. The harmonious color scheme for the last ten years has been the most popular color scheme and is, indeed, the easiest with which to achieve success because the effect is one of richness without disturbance to the chief color. Related colors used together are interesting in themselves, so you needn't work overtime to introduce attractive accessories or textures. Harmony is also nature's favorite color scheme. If you look out of a picture window in the country, you discover a harmonious color scheme, from yellowish green to bluish green in the distant trees and mountains, and the blue in the sky. Think of a sunset. Its colors appear on the other side of the color chart: yellow, orange, red, purple, and finally black at night; not one color has been left out, each in succession, right on down the chart, as the sun fades.

Today the contrasting color scheme is fast coming into popularity. Full contrasts are composed of colors opposite each other on the color chart, such as yellow and purple. Unlike harmonious colors, they are as far removed from each other as colors can be. Nature is not very fond of using full contrasts, at least not in large quantities. And people too find them difficult to put together, often reserving their use for the important holidays, when we wish to cause an impact. At Christmas, for instance, we use red and green; at Easter, yellow and purple. For Thanksgiving, we use the harvest colors, harmonious colors that nature puts together. In the late summer and fall her colors are the harmonious combinations of rust, orange and gold. When we think of spring flowers, the bright pastels of pink, lavender and blue come to mind. Man may mix colors in a potpourri in his garden, but when nature is left alone she is usually harmonious.

It is difficult to use contrasting colors together effectively for the interior of the home because the result may be too jarring or tiring. There are, however, ways to make the result inviting. You can use contrasting colors that have been grayed down a bit from nature's full color. Then the colors become related through the common denominator of gray, and thus become more in agreement with each other.

Or you might use one color far more than any other. This is nature's favorite way of using contrasting colors. Surrounding the rose bush is a predominance of green. The same can be said of holly berries in winter. Contrasting colors dominate and thus have a way of competing with each other. Putting them together in somewhat equal amounts is like having two heads of government, two attractive women trying to outshine each other at a party, or two comedians struggling to be the more humorous on a television show. After a while it becomes taxing. So if you use blue and orange together, use a great deal of blue, for instance, and only a small amount of orange.

A third way to use contrasting colors together is to combine what is called reduced contrasts. Instead of putting exact opposites together, use a color found on either side of one of the contrasts. Don't use blue and orange, but blue and yellow or blue and red. Blue and yellow are favorites in combination right now, and wherever Oriental rugs are used we find blue and red completely satisfying for furniture fabrics. These colors are closer in relationship and therefore are more compatible.

The fourth and most popular way of using contrasting colors together is in a print. In the last ten years, prints have been somewhat out of style. When the shorter sofa returned in popularity, the print came back into its own again, and with it came the contrasting color scheme. If we have a design or pattern with which we identify, using contrasting colors sprinkled around the rest of the room makes sense. Then they have a reason for being. Take, for instance, red and green. If used without a design, red and green together would not be harmonious and you might wonder why these two colors were chosen to go with each other. But put a print of red flowers with green leaves on the sofa, and the two colors in similar amounts used throughout the rest of the room seem correct. It is an easy way to decorate because, no matter what the colors are, the outcome is unified. Introducing a print immediately establishes the color scheme of a room.

Do not forget that strong splashes of color can be exciting in small amounts, but tedious in large amounts or when they must be endured for long periods of time. But you can have fun with a jumble of eight brilliant colors, practically the whole rainbow. Once I decorated a garden-type room that had a white tile floor and white walls with a smart potpourri print that almost shrieked, it was so loud. It covered a deep-tufted sofa loaded down with pillows representing all the colors in the print. For the two card tables in the room, the eight chairs were upholstered each in a different color taken from the print. Each of the four lounge chairs sported a different wild color. The furniture covers were tied together by the dominating print on the sofa. With walls of glass looking out into the garden, the use of many inside plants, most of them massive, and a large aviary, this room was a striking foil for a party. The outdoor lighting was extremely well planned so that there was no need to close the white draperies at night. But remember that a conglomerate color scheme that does not soon become tiring is not easy to achieve. If you are not sure of your use of color, the safest method is to follow nature and use the color the way she does.

Discord, or reversing the natural order of the relative strength of colors, is not endurable in large masses, but sometimes in small quantities it can add brilliance to a room. Too much sweetness or too much smoothness seems to annoy human beings. We like surprizes. A discordant note may be introduced by a picture, flowers, vase or sofa pillows.

The intensity of color is tremendously affected by climate. As a teacher, I am always being asked if it isn't wrong to use yellow in a southwest exposure or blue in a northern one. In sections of the country having extremes of temperature for many months out of the year, extreme suggestions of climate are inappropriate for interior coloring. I would not particularly like a hot gold on the walls of a living room facing the southwest in Georgia or an icy blue bedroom wall facing northeast in Maine.

Perhaps the most delightful color scheme can be had by keying all the leading colors to one dominant color. For example, in using a combination of red and blue, with red dominating, blue is more successful if it tends toward purple rather than green because it becomes closer in its relation to red this way. The large areas in a room, such as the walls, floors and draperies, should be keyed in this manner, whereas small areas need not be. If the sofa is not keyed to the wall behind, the whole room may appear unmatched. Yet if a small occasional chair is not keyed to the dominant color, it does not necessarily spoil the room.

Because some people are not aware of the relationship of colors, they select the wrong neutral background to go with the other colors in their rooms. An off-white, to look good with red, blue or purple, should be tinted slightly rose beige. One chosen for orange, gold, or green looks far better tinted a sandy beige. Most off-whites today reflect either yellow or red. The difference is so subtle that a person who has a gold sofa backed up to a wall of white with a suggestion of rose beige in it may not understand what is wrong with his living room. If the sofa is orange, however, the result is fine. Since orange is the color between yellow and red, it can be used advantageously with either off-white tint.

The value, or amount of light or dark, of a color should be considered, too. As you must realize, if you wish to minimize the size or shape of an object it should be exactly the same color as the background. Just covering, in any shade of green, a fat ugly sofa that sits against a pale green wall would not do the trick. It, too, should be upholstered with the same pale green. It does not have to be the same color—it could be another color of the same value as the wall and the result would be almost as effective. If an unattractive chest in a room of reds and blues were painted red and sat against a pale pink wall, the chest would stand out more sharply than Jimmy Durante in a daisy chain, but if it were painted pale blue it would be much less noticeable.

If a room is done in only one or two colors, the best effect can be achieved through the use of many degrees in the values of the colors. For instance, with green you might wish to use three values: celery, green almond and moss green. As more colors are used in a room, smartness depends on keeping the values within one color very much the same, or the result becomes a hodgepodge.

I am constantly confronted by the timid soul with the question: "How many colors should I use in my room?" The answer, of course, depends entirely on the individual, but if you feel unsure of yourself it would probably be best to pick out one dominant color and use one or two other colors in lesser degrees. A reduced contrasting color scheme could include blue with red and touches of turquoise. A harmonizing color scheme, on the other hand, could combine orange with yellow and red as a minor note. It is rewarding to be able to go into a room and instantly be aware of one outstanding color. This notion gives emphasis to a room and creates a feeling of unity. If color is not planned, the resulting effect can be just as confusing as poorly arranged furniture.

Color should be well distributed throughout a room because we can create balance through color. One should be particularly careful with deep values of any color, since a weight problem can easily occur.

If the problem of color is causing wrinkles on your otherwise smooth brow, try this simple formula. Use neutral colors for your large areas, more intense colors for your upholstered pieces, and still brighter hues for your accessories and small areas. Loud colors on walls overwhelm any soft pastels found in a room. Such walls call for equally loud colors on furniture, or at least good strong whites. Attention must be given to the reverse scheme. Brilliant colors in the room don't do a thing for pastel walls. Here, white or wood finishes look best.

There is no need to accent unimportant places in a room with intense colors unless for balance. One room I sought to change had a peculiar nook, too small to be of much use, at one side of the living room. The lady of the house thought it should be spruced up and painted it bright red. It was a mistake for it now became the dominating feature in the room.

Color has tremendous power, more control over us than we imagine. Blue might be soothing for one person, yet make another feel depressed. Color lends itself to psychological motivation. It stirs emotions. Most people have preferences, which sometimes run in the families. After years of questioning my classes about their color preferences, I have found out that most women are guided in choosing colors for their homes by two factors: the area in the United States in which they live and the colors currently being pushed by the leading magazines. Blue was surprisingly low in favor in California until just recently. Now it appears to be taking the place of the once popular orange, although green and yellow are still coholders of first place.

Of course, color preferences change with age. For a young child, it is almost always red; although we may never lose our love for red, we become more subtle in our color partialities with age. You who feel a three-year-old child should help decorate his room be forewarned. Red will be his choice. For a rugged boy, this choice would be perfect, but not for a girl. Her love for red can be more than satisfied with a fire-engine red toy or two. Twenty years ago I had as a client a supposedly modern mother. Her beautiful blond girl of three came along to pick out the materials for her room. The child's endearing personality would suggest pale pinks and blues, but those colors bored her. Her interest was in a wild circus print of red and green. So we did her room in red and green, and it was entirely out of keeping with her. The room was much more suited for her seven-year-old brother, who was a perfect devil. Yet she kept this room until she was ten, at which time she had enough sense to realize that it was all wrong for her.

One apologetic mother opened the door to a bedroom to show me what her little son had picked out for his wall color. The whole room was blazing in the brightest yellow I have ever seen. I thought for a split second that something had happened to the sun. I am sure that boy did not need a night light. The room must have glowed even in the darkness. The boy had picked the color from a small color chip. He had no idea of how it would look on the ceiling and four walls.

I am constantly dumbfounded why women, who are unsure of their own decorating abilities, allow their children to have complete freedom in choosing color and furniture for their rooms. The young ones may think they know what they like, but they have no ability to picture the result while they are putting a room together. If your child shows no interest in planning his room, don't push it. You can now take the place of a decorator and plan his room attractively according to his tastes.

The psychological effects of color are fascinating. Consider the basic colors. Red can be easily overused, and can create too intense an atmosphere, so it should be used guardedly. If you investigate its different hues, though, red is probably not a bad choice of color for the dining room for the reason that we use this room infrequently, so it should appear to be lively to keep the conversation scintillating. But a brilliant red living room would generally be poor because a great deal of time is spent in quiet pursuits there.

Guests' bathrooms and the powder room might be fun in red, as long as there is plenty of white or black to relieve the intensity. To me, bathrooms should have a cool, refreshing quality about them and are therefore not at their best when decorated in hot, heavy colors. One hot June day I saw an inside bathroom that was done completely in red, even the towels. Humorous black and white prints hanging on the walls provided the only color break in the room. The effect was one of oppressive heat.

I decorated one bathroom that had many red touches in it, yet was so overwhelmingly white that it appeared as refreshing as a Swiss postcard. The floor and fixtures were white. On the walls above the white tile trimmed in black was a white-background wallpaper with a wide basket weave done in indefinite black lines. The only large wall space was occupied by a large abstract painting in reds, black and white. The towels and rugs were red, as well as the coarsely woven linen draperies. Placed on the counter top was a handsome black vase holding red roses. There is no doubt that plants or flowers in a bathroom help soften its rigid feeling, particularly when it is predominantly white. A bunch of roses in a small room gives off a fragrance that is exceptionally pleasing.

Although using red as the main color in a kitchen would be a relief from the usual yellow, I would be careful not to overdo it. To be constantly working on a red counter top might be tiring on the eyes. Be careful not to use red too much in any popular room in the house.

Blue is just the opposite. It is the coldest looking color, soothing to excitable people and depressing to others. If your child is difficult to settle down at night, you might try a pleasant blue in his bedroom and see if it helps.

Blue is the most difficult color in the decorator's workbook because it is greatly influenced by other colors. If you are planning to decorate a room primarily in blue, you are going to have to work to match all the blues properly. Most people seem to prefer the turquoise side of the color chart to blue-violet. If you decide to use a soft blue, be sure to check the color at night because so often a quiet blue turns gray at night, and what might be a lovely effect during the day can be swallowed up entirely at dusk. If you are the owner of some eighteenth-century English wood pieces in reddish brown mahogany, you cannot do better than to use a soft blue as one of your main colors. A gentle color, it sets off the richness of the wood.

Yellow gives us all the feeling of warmth and cheerfulness. It is known as the color of the happiest emotion. Women like it for the kitchen because it starts off their day right. It is an unoffensive color.

Yellow is really at its best when bright, although two other values of yellow are used extensively. The first, chartreuse, must be handled with care, because when used in large amounts it can become too much. With some thought, its application can be chic and captivating. The second value often used is mustard. Mix it with harmonious colors of the right hue and it is ever so smart. Mustard is a favorite color in the sunshine states.

Gold has a richness that mustard lacks and is at its best in metal, gilt, or silk. Unfortunately, cottons and most synthetic fabrics come out not gold but a rather dull mustard. Gold in metal has the brightness of silver, plus warmth, and there is hardly a room alive, no matter what the color scheme, that isn't improved with the introduction of gold in this medium. In an elaborate decor, nothing can be so lovely as a silk fabric in gold, for it sparkles with depth and richness. Gold foil wallpaper and gold silk gauze curtains at a window dress up a bathroom as nothing else can.

Green produces the most normal reaction in people because it is associated with nature. It is said that if you hate green you are neurotic because, in hating it, you are not accepting the world as it is. The most refreshing and restful of colors, green is good for warm climates and country houses. Except in the range of bright Kelly green, it is not a sophisticated color, so it rarely finds its way congenially into large city apartments.

Two values of green are very successful in the right environment. One is Nile green, an exquisitely pale green that has a silvery quality about it. In a traditional atmosphere creating a background for rich mahogany furniture, satin fabrics, silver and crystal ornaments, nothing could be more beautiful. It is the type of color that should be used in the temperate zones of the United States. Its beauty is lost in the glaring light of the brilliant sunshine of our western states.

The other hue is the popular yellow-green that we will call olive green. Wherever an expanse of glass shows off a carefully watered patio area that stays green all year around, this color becomes a joy to behold as the main color scheme for a living room. The indoor-outdoor effect that it helps to create harmonizes living space. One of the nicest tricks is to use a deep pile, grassy green area rug that gives the appearance of actually bringing into the room the grass outside. If the glass goes to the floor and we use lots of inside plants, who is to say where the inside stops and the outside begins?

Green is not always the answer to a housewife's prayer. It can become heavy and sticky, as happens when whole rooms are covered with a dull, medium green. Without the relief of lots of white, these rooms are depressing. Now that this lacquer green is returning to popularity, I hope it will be sensibly used in conjunction with many vivid colors.

I am reminded of a story a student told me about green ceilings. In the student's social group was one lady who just loved to entertain, and in fact had the knack of giving great parties. Naturally, they all loved going to her parties, except for one thing. Her living room, with white walls, had a heavy green ceiling and all the women looked ghastly under this canopy. One day they were discussing this situation at a bridge party she happened to miss, and they decided to go in a body and suggest that she repaint her ceiling. They did, and she was delighted with the idea, immediately suggesting a painting party. When the party was in full swing, the ladies suddenly realized that she was sitting down in a covered up lounge chair having the time of her life, directing, but not budging one iota. The party went on for some time because green is the hardest color to cover up. It always needs one more coat than any other color. At least the ladies were gratified that their friend's parties were even greater successes from that time on. Paint your ceilings anything but green.

Orange has the invigorating reactions of both red and yellow, and is an extremely cheerful color. For the majority of people, its warmth and vibrance are often too stimulating, at least in large amounts. If you happen to live in a contemporary house with plywood walls, you cannot do better than to use orange for your color scheme. It is handsome with most woods because of their brown cast, and brown is orange with black added. It blends with wood, yet perks it up. Pale colors have as much chance of survival surrounded by wood walls as a tray of French pastries in a room full of fat ladies.

Orange is a modern color, at least to the western world. It came to us from the Orient, where it had an illustrious past. Actually, we became aware of it about the time the movie *The King and I* was released. The brilliant colors flashing on and off through that film opened up a whole new world of color for us, and orange took its place at the top of the list. We now find it the most successful color in the sunshine states, particularly those in which desert scenery rules design. Poor with mahogany and mulberry tones, it is at its best with woods—especially walnut, teak, or oak—and with gold and olive green.

Purple is a color of an entirely different mood. All colors change in mood as they range from pale to dark tones, but purple appears to change its mood most. Purple gives the impression of dignity and reserve because it is so cold and austere.

Back in style now, it is far more popular in its pastel tints and has been a favorite among the six-to-sixteen set for some time. A good choice, too, because there is something sweet and feminine, slightly more sophisticated than pink, about lavender. Be careful using lavender, though, because it can so easily cause discord if not combined with the proper colors. If it is a flower print with green leaves, it looks right with green; but without a print, play it safe and combine it with blue or pink of equal or less intensity.

White with purple, as with red, is extremely successful. Since purple spreads a certain sense of gloom, anything metallic gold is also excellent with it. Both purple and gilt denote richness anyway, and the warmth and glitter of gold fits in with the high tone of a purple scheme. Purple is not often used in the living room, but is usually reserved for the bedroom.

Black has a tremendous amount of character, but in large amounts it can be depressing unless it is shiny. Every now and then, you come across a person who insists on using black for most of the walls in her home. She is usually sophisticated, and generally lives in an apartment. The result is a night club atmosphere.

Black is extremely successful as an accent color. Nothing will set off a diamond more than a piece of black velvet. If you are particularly anxious to display accessories, you cannot do better than to place them on a black lacquered chest or shelf. Almost any room, traditional or contemporary, can take a piece of black furniture. Black is smart in woods, tile, and velvet fabrics. Black needs the pile weaves or leather effects to be truly handsome for furniture coverings. So often both dad's chair and the love seat in the den or family room are black. It seems to be practical for dad because it appears masculine, the opposite of virginal white, and its lack of identity makes it fit in almost any color scheme. There are also some handsome black and white print fabrics on the market that would be great in a room with lots of white and touches of red.

White denotes purity and lightness, and like black it has the ability to make adjacent colors more interesting. We are passing through the end of a long period of preference for this color, particularly for the shell of a room. There is no doubt about it. With the advent of brilliant colors, white becomes the perfect background to set them off. Put a strong lime green against a beige wall, and you have nothing; change the wall color to white, and the effect is smart.

White gives a clean, expansive look of richness and is a perfect foil for any of the lovely colors to be used in accessories. On the other hand, white is not always the easiest color to coordinate. There are 275 different values of white, and they have a way of affecting each other. If not carefully chosen, a clear, brilliant white can make others seem either dirty or old. White-background wallpaper can actually look yellowed next to a new candlewick bedspread.

The neutral color gray is seen so often. It is most popular in the sections of the United States where there are many gray days. How soft colors are on gray days! Often associated with unhappy love affairs in popular songs, we consider a gray day a dismal day, and when it is used in the home we tend to feel the same way about it. Its coldness must be warmed up by the use of yellow, orange or red, the so-called hot colors. Pale pink, apricot, and soft yellow are exquisite when introduced into a gray background. So often we hear it is wrong to use blue or purple with gray because gray is gloomy enough without further help. It is true that in their full intensity blue and purple are not very satisfying with gray, but if they are softened they add loveliness. If you have ever had the chance to view the Atlantic Ocean in the early evening, you have seen how well nature places them together.

Gray is presently out of favor for home furnishings. For some reason, gray dye does not make the most of itself with cotton or synthetic fabrics, although it lends itself handsomely to paint or wool. Since it is neutral, it makes the perfect background color for almost any room. It is in the same category as white, only softer, less vibrant. Old hands and heads are not afraid to use it.

Wood painted gray can be lovely, and today a wood patina of rubbed-off gray, perhaps showing a silver trim, is ever so smart. For you who like French Provincial bedroom furniture, gray might be a pleasant change from the usual white with a gold trim.

Silver gives off a gray cast. Although we may be tired of gray tiles in the bathroom, their ability to fit the shining chrome of the fixtures makes them successful. Bathrooms are generally such small areas that they are not at their best combining silvery chrome with gold accessories. Since most bathroom accessories are manufactured in gold, gold fixtures have been on the rise in the last few years. Unfortunately, these are a lot more care for the housewife than the old-fashioned chrome ones. If you must combine the chrome and gilt, install a smart foil wallpaper of both gold and silver; like the print for the contrasting color scheme, the chrome and gilt should then fit together.

Brown has never been too popular in home decorations except with people of a very practical turn of mind. Unfortunately, their only consideration is usually in creating an interior that does not show the dirt, and thus they lose the open invitation to create rooms of beauty. Brown can be lovely if treated correctly. Always smart with white, it is a delight with pink, red on the orange side, pale blue, yellow, gold and of course any value of orange, since it is a shade of orange itself. It is terrible with purple, but all right with green if the brown is a yellow-brown and the green also leans toward that side of the color chart. A rich, reddish brown with a strong medium green is a failure because they are almost contrasting colors and are too heavy for each other. Brown doesn't do much for mahogany furniture, either, although the color is chic with oak or walnut.

Dark brown walls can be used in a library if white woodwork and many colorful books are used to create a contrast. In a boy's bedroom, brown walls are interesting with tan furniture and burlap draperies. The bedspread can be a tweed of brown and tan.

To use brown as the main color in a living room, it would be particularly effective to have walls of glass through which the eye can be drawn to a group of tree trunks. To keep the room light, the walls should be white with well-polished, dark oak floors and deep-piled white area rugs. The upholstered furniture can be covered with a dark, yellow-brown linen cover with a large pattern etched in white. More white can come into the room with a skirted table and white sofa pillows. Burnt orange and gold bring relief in the accessories. The result is a color scheme not duplicated everywhere up and down the street.

Except for brown, I have not been discussing separately the tints and shades of the various colors, but I do think pink warrants a little consideration for its very different mood from the mother color, red. Pink has a clean, fresh quality about it that through the ages has given a strong impression of being little-girlish or boudoirish. Yet, the last twenty years, it has come away from its feminine role to be found in any room in the house. Some husbands object violently to it and feel that if the master bedroom is mostly in pink they have been thrust into a sissy atmosphere that might encroach upon their masculinity. In that thought alone is an unconscious display of the power of color. If pink is used with heavier colors, it can lose its wishy-washy character and settle down to make a room of great beauty. Try it in a living room with navy (a rarely used color for interiors) and camelia red. Use it in the master bedroom with a good heavy brown. Pink kitchens can be refreshing, too, if they are not overdone. Pink, but not too pink. It might be particularly enjoyable in a kitchen that, because of poor ventilation, has a way of being too hot. Naturally, it will never go out of style for bathrooms, especially if the tile is gray, and there isn't a little girl in the world who doesn't look like a dream child in a sweet pink room.

If you are unsure of yourself on color, start collecting pictures of rooms that appeal to you. Remember experiences you have enjoyed in which color had a part. Was it a particular chiffon evening dress of your youth? Was it the sudden view of a lake as you rounded a bend on a high mountain trail? Was it the spreading peacock's tail you saw at the zoo as a child? Do you dream in color? If so, do particular colors keep recurring? When you are ready to decorate, go back over all this and you will probably find that certain colors appeal to you more than others. Don't be afraid of color, or you will end up with mediocrity. It doesn't have to shout at you, but be open-minded about it. Remember the few hints I have given you so that you can easily make your room a success. The walls and floors are actually the most important areas because they contain so much space to be covered. You can start anywhere with color. If you decide that you wish to use a print, by all means start with it because now your color scheme has been established and the rest of the way should be fairly easy. Without a print you may use for your inspiration almost anything, such as a painting, an unusual rug, wallpaper, an afghan, a Chinese vase, a bedspread, a wall hanging, a screen, a dried flower arrangement that is to be a focal point in the room, and so on. If all this leaves you completely blank, then perhaps you had better start with the rug or wall-to-wall carpet because the manufacturers offer the least variety of colors in this commodity.

If you are planning to use wallpaper, do try to get the sample book home to see your choice in the room in which you plan to use it. It is hard to get the full impact at the store surrounded by hundreds of samples. What might look gay and fun in a small sample may be a shrieking horror over four walls, so close your eyes and try to imagine the design multiplied a hundred times. If it is already very lively, beware!

Many people do their own inside painting. Do not wait for that morning your husband bounces out of bed and says, "This is the day I paint the living room." Make sure you have the right color first.

Any paint store manager will tell you the color you have on the little swatch is going to change drastically after the paint is placed on the wall. Make the drying test and settle with your color expert before you give hubby the brush. A color on a swatch looks about three times brighter when it is spread all over a wall, except for off-whites, which tend to appear lighter. Of all the paint colors, blue appears to be the one with the most surprizes, so watch it carefully. Buy it toned down. A terra-cotta patio outside a sliding glass door will change the paint noticeably from the way it looked in the yellow light at the paint store. Even an abundance of greenery through a window will drive you crazy trying to maintain your desired effect. So when you buy your paint, buy it from a store whose pleasure it is to help its clients out of these dilemmas.

When a wall is pastel, the whole room, including ceiling and woodwork, can be painted the same color. As the wall color becomes darker, it is much safer to paint the ceiling and woodwork white to keep the room from looking like a cave. Excessively bright or dark colors need the relief of white. This rule holds true no matter in what circumstance you use color. On the other hand, pastels often function better with soft off-whites rather than with a glaring white.

Although white certainly helps to increase the feeling of space, blue is the best color of all because we unconsciously relate soft blue to the infinite space of the sky. So if you are truly interested in creating the feeling of space, try light blue.

In a tiny house or apartment it might be well to paint almost all the walls the same color in order to give the sense of unity and expansiveness needed in closed-in areas. How far should you continue with one color scheme throughout an average-sized house? A three-bedroom house would certainly be monotonous if there were no change of colors throughout. However, as a symphony repeats a central theme, one color could be shown in different shades and amounts through the main rooms of the home. Such repetition does not necessarily have to occur in the children's rooms, which may be little castles unto themselves. Orange, for instance, could be the main color combined with white in the kitchen. In the living room and dining room it could be used with gold and olive green, turning to apricot and gray in the master bedroom and bath, with heavy brown, white and orange in the den. Then there would be a unified flow of colors throughout the main areas of the house. As you walk through a home it is disconcerting to step from one bright color scheme into another, none of them related in any way. The worst fault of all, of course, is to go from one strong color to another in wall-to-wall carpeting. I have hit as many as five drastic changes in carpet color in one house. The effect of such variety is not the same when rugs are used and a wood floor unifies the whole.

Ceilings at times can be considered in your color scheme. Most ceilings should not attract attention, but occasionally painting a ceiling can be quite effective. In a stately dining room, I once had a coved ceiling painted sky blue. It was effective because the room had two French doors that led the eye out onto some blue mountains and up to the sky. On the side walls above a dado was placed a dignified flower-and-bird print to harmonize with the garden beyond the terrace. Since ordinarily so little wall space shows in the kitchen, I have continued the lattice paper right up over the ceiling, giving the kitchen the effect of a gazebo. Another time, in a boy's room with white walls, I had the ceiling as well as the space between two windows against which the double bed was placed painted tangerine to bring out the main color in a vivid scroll that hung on the wall over the headboard. And what could be sweeter in a little girl's room than nosegay wallpaper extending over the ceiling to make a bower of rosebuds? But nothing is more distressing than to see wallpaper placed on a kitchen ceiling, slowly bearing down on the occupants. To be correct in this case, the same paper should be repeated on at least one wall in the kitchen or breakfast nook. Remember, we prefer the "growth upwards" idea, not "the sky is falling" look. These are just a few suggestions of what may be done. Never forget that the ceiling is an integral part of the room.

It is fashionable to show wood floors again. The wood should be dark in tone, for we have discovered it is by far a more handsome foil for today's clear colors than were the shiny, postwar orange-finished ones. Kept polished, a modern hardwood floor generally calls for rugs, room-size or area. Just the way a small sofa may wear a livelier coat than a huge one, area rugs can be far fancier than wall-to-wall carpeting. So you can see we now must pick our floor covering with great care, making sure it will become an integral part of the room. The design need not be as complicated as that found in Oriental rugs, just a beautiful color with an interesting texture.

In the warmer areas in the United States, tiles are often used throughout a house. Unlike hardwood floors, tiles do not necessarily need rugs. But tile alone creates a cold look that is best softened by the use of many plants and accessories. A tile that is used consistently throughout a house should be somewhat neutral—white, gray, beige or Spanish Red—because it is so permanent. On the other hand, I live with a pale, olive green tile throughout a house in California and like it very much. And I once saw a neutral tile laid throughout a home except in the dining room where a tile riotous with bouquets of flowers was used. It was charming in the dining room because the many large, wood pieces alone would have tended to cause dullness.

For a last few tips on color, remember that men generally prefer dramatic colorings with intense conflicts and splashy effects, so any room that is for their exclusive use could be planned to include brilliant or deep colors. Decide on the personality of the person whose room you are decorating and use a color scheme that is best for him. In rooms in which you do not spend a great deal of time, be daring in using color combinations. Some colors, such as the greens, yellows and oranges, look best in a country setting, whereas reds, purples, grays, blacks and whites go well with the formal setting of city life. Dark shades are more restful than light tints. If you live on a noisy street, you may find that the addition of dark colors in the rooms on the street side can make a restful haven where no such feeling could have existed before.

At any rate, have fun and enjoy your use of color. It is all around us and is one of the few remaining joys that is absolutely free.

Furniture Arrangements

ɞ **5**

Furniture arrangement is primarily concerned with comfort, although style and beauty are also basic essentials. We may use furniture from the past, but we rarely duplicate the furniture arrangement of any particular period because our social activities call for something different. The arrangement of furniture reflects the activities and cultural interests of the family.

Fundamentally, furniture arranging is a problem in floor composition, and one of the best ways of solving it is by drawing to scale the room and its furniture. Although the resulting picture may not be complete or final, it saves the wear and tear on muscles and on tempers that arise when furniture is moved about a room in search of a resting place. Having a floor plan is particularly helpful if you own a grand piano, which is a move-once item as far as most husbands are concerned. Unfortunately, sometimes even the best measured drawings can be wrong, so use yours with a fluid mind. After all, a measured drawing is a flat composition, and when the arrangement is seen in its three-dimensional reality the result may be less pleasant. While you are working with your little scaled pieces, therefore, try to visualize how the furniture will appear upright in the room. It may be that those two wing chairs will block most of the view from your window if they were placed in front of it with a table and a fat lamp in between.

Then, too, we cannot always foresee how certain patterns in living occur until we actually have lived in a room for a short time. It may be that you have just the spot for a desk in your living room, but if you do not really have enough seating space the desk must go so that the living room may function correctly. Perhaps on the measured drawing it appears that the space in the living room warrants only a small chow table for a coffee table. If you entertain constantly and that entertaining consists of a great deal of conversation and many refreshments, it is probably better to use up some of the precious floor space and have a coffee table large enough to take all the food and dishes.

The most important commodities you buy in a house are the floor space and the layout of the rooms. You can change color schemes, but if you have to alter the walls, unless renovating old houses is your hobby, the house is the wrong one for you. I would not consider buying a house until I had at least made a measured drawing of the living room and master bedroom because these are the rooms in which the greatest problems in arrangement seem to occur. You who move with nine-foot sofas, grand pianos and stereo cabinets must not guess about their placement in a future home. It all should be down in black and white on a measured drawing before you sign on the dotted line. One of my students fell in love with a color scheme, and when she moved into the poorly planned living room she found she had to block off one of the many doors with her tremendous sectional sofa; if anyone played the piano when a fire was burning in the fireplace, he got a hot seat. There is more than one house for you, but unfortunately we women are so emotional about house buying that we are likely to have instant love affairs with them.

It makes me sick at heart to see a young couple move into their first house from an apartment and find that their master bedroom does not accommodate the handsome bedroom furniture they recently acquired. I do not know what is wrong with contractors, but they seem to have trouble realizing that today in America the king-size bed reigns supreme, along with its coordinate, the triple dresser. You who have not yet invested in some good bedroom furniture and expect to be moving frequently during your married life should buy furniture that takes height, such as the armoire and lingerie chest, so that you have fewer worries with space problems.

Even before you start house hunting, write your requirements down in order to have some idea of how they fit into an imaginary room. You may in that way prevent a disastrous love affair with the wrong house.

Since each room has its own problems, I am pushed into a corner to give general rules on arrangements that may fit all cases. As you can easily see, a living room has little in common with a bedroom. The distribution of furniture should be fairly even so that one end does not seem more crowded than another; otherwise, the room appears uncomfortable, insecure, and it strains your sense of balance. Opposite walls should be similarly furnished or should at least appear evenly balanced in number of pieces. Thus the favorite old standby is so correct: a sofa and chairs opposite a fireplace that is flanked by chairs. Large pieces of furniture look best parallel to the walls of the room. It is almost impossible to achieve unity when everything is diagonally placed. Do not forget that dark colors have more weight than pale ones and that allover patterns reduce size just the way army camouflaging hides shapes. Remember that balance should be achieved in a free and easy manner, just the way nature achieves an allover balance in the outline of a perfect tree without duplicating one branch within the tree itself.

There are inherent problems in arranging furniture and accessories in a high-low pattern against a wall. Every now and then, you see a room that gives you the impression that horizontal bands are running around all four walls, because everything seems to be of the same height. This fault occurs most frequently in a contemporary home that offers little chance for average windows and single doorways to produce a high-low effect. A high back chair, whether a wing chair or an interesting rocker, is a great help in disrupting this line. Breakfronts and secretaries, which have recently reappeared on the style scene, can come to the rescue to relieve this impression.

If your room suffers from a wall of glass for windows, a wall of brick for the fireplace and a wide opening into the room for a door-

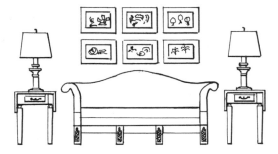

way, create the high-low look with pictures. You could place pictures over the sofa higher than the lamps on each side. If you hang prints on each side of a breakfront, do not deaden the composition by ending the prints on the same line as the top of the breakfront. This time, because the breakfront is a high piece, the pictures should stop lower down. At any rate, look around your living room to see if the eye travels from high to low and back again, because the emphasis today, regardless of the long chests found in living rooms, dining rooms and bedrooms, is on the vertical, not on the horizontal.

We might also dwell for a moment on the use of pairs. Undoubtedly, it is not the preferred way to set up a living room today, but matching furniture unifies a room. Some rooms are more flattering when the appearance of one chair is distinguished by its twin nearby. Yet a housewife sensitive to harmony might easily overdo it because too many twins in a room cause a lack of spontaneity. A twin or two in chairs, end tables or lamps helps avoid the jumbled effect resulting when nothing is matched. Remember that the patchwork quilt was sewed out of scraps to save money, not to produce a work of art.

Now, getting down to the individual room, it is necessary for you to think about its arrangement. It goes beyond just pretty patterns in a rectangle on a piece of paper. What room is it? What is its function as a whole? What will be the further requirements of this room because it belongs to you? What pieces of furniture are necessary in order to carry out its functions properly? How best may it be done so that the occupants, both family and guests, may find themselves in a happy room?

Our first concern is the living room. Most women go to a great deal of trouble and put a large amount of money into making this room attractive and then fail to use it. What is the primary purpose of a living room? Although the family certainly should use it, we know it must primarily be the entertainment room for guests. The frequency and type of entertainment, then, would be important considerations.

Some people limit their entertaining to bridge. For such people, a permanently set-up bridge table would be a must, followed by enough easy-to-clear space for two more tables. A huge, heavy coffee table could be unwieldy, in which event I would suggest instead one or two small coffee squares placed by the sofa.

Other people like to give intimate dinners for four to six people, followed by long hours of conversation in the living room. In this case, the sofa becomes all-important and should have comfortable chairs on either side and easy-to-move chairs situated in other parts

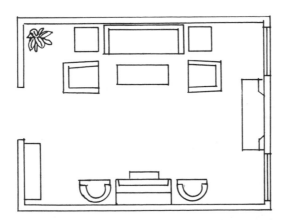

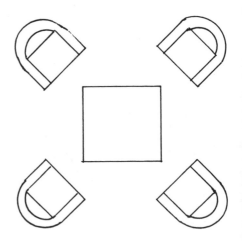

of the room, such as on each side of a stereo. A large coffee table could take its place as a center piece for the group. This arrangement is also excellent for all the meetings you housewives hold in your homes.

An extremely chic arrangement for this type of entertaining is a huge round or square coffee table set in front of the fireplace surrounded by four comfortable lounge chairs sitting on the diagonal in the room. If three couples constitute the company for the evening, two occasional chairs can easily find their way into the group as well.

It has been discovered that round or octagonal tables make the best type of conference table because when human beings are lined up opposite each other at a rectangular table they automatically take sides like armies ready for battle. So perhaps a round table is ideal for pleasant conversation.

A somewhat new member to the furniture world is the party table, designed especially for an evening of conversation and refreshments. Of continental table height (about 25 inches) and large diameter, it takes up a good deal of space in a corner. Some women prefer to use it as a dining table when their dining ells are completely exposed to the living room, trying to disguise the fact that this corner is actually the dining room. I do not blame them for this attitude, but the seemingly clever idea has two faults: first, long legged people are miserable eating a whole meal at anything less than normal dining table height; second, few of them extend for leaves, making them extremely limited for the number they can serve. Also, although good for poker, they are a little too large for comfortable bridge playing.

For those who entertain large groups for dinner, a buffet dinner

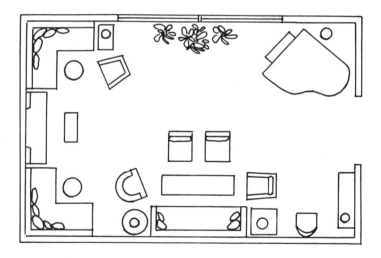

becomes a necessity. For this there should be about three different seating groups in the living room because there is a limit on how large a group can carry on one conversation. Four is a perfect number. Certainly, six is the limit.

The chaise lounge is returning to favor to aid the housewife in the problem of seating space. Because the chaise lounge is open on three sides, it can be stuffed three deep with guests who enjoy moving from one group to another. Benches, ottomans, stacking stools, and, for the very young, floor pillows can also complete a flexible scene. Floor pillows are a temporary measure to be brought out when all other sitting spaces are filled. It is wise to survey the ruins at the end of a party to see exactly what your guests have done to your furniture arrangement. If, party after party, a certain form of rearrangement consistently occurs, study your arrangement for deficiencies.

On the other hand, perhaps you and your friends like to sing and dance or just listen to music and tape recordings. If it is singing you like, there should be plenty of space around the piano. With the twinkle toes group, area rugs should be the choice for floor coverings since they can be easily rolled up. It is unnecessary to have a whole room arranged for stereo listening unless this activity is your main pleasure. The stereo should then take the focal position that the fireplace usually commands so that the sofa group against the opposite wall is in the perfect location for listening.

Then there are those who entertain only once in a great while with a big cocktail party. Since this social activity makes its own rules, I would not worry about a furniture arrangement. I cannot remember a cocktail party in which I felt the arrangement of the rooms made it a success. Fix your living room to suit your family's needs.

Now that we have sent the company on its way home at last, we can make the living room the right room for you. The best spot for the sofa is along the longest wall, where the space offers plenty of room for end tables, a coffee table, lounge chairs and almost anything else. It also is a natural for balancing the fireplace, which is usually opposite. If your fireplace is somewhat off center (I am not talking about corner fireplaces), center your sofa directly opposite it. Do not place the sofa in the center of its wall, or the room will look lopsided.

Since our social life has pushed the conversational evening to the fore, we have discovered a pleasant way to arrange for this activity: the conversation island. It has become very popular today to bring short sofas, not over seven feet long, out from the fireplace wall. There can be just one sofa with lounge chairs opposite. There can be

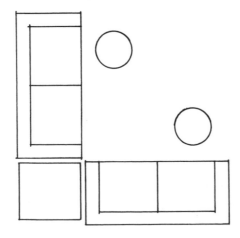

two sofas with a large square or round coffee table in between and occasional chairs at the end on the diagonal facing the fireplace; or there can be two sofas, perhaps one seven feet and the other five feet long, making a sectional effect with a square table at the corner instead of the 1950 upholstered curved piece. The long sofa is no longer used.

Sometimes the sofa is placed in the middle of the room, facing a fireplace that shares with the sofa the two good lounge chairs, one on each side. If the sofa is too long, it does not measure up well to the

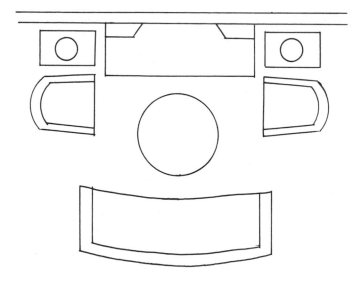

fireplace opening. The chairs at its side either stand too far away from the fireplace or extend into the sofa area. Thus, a six-foot sofa or a five-foot love seat is best for this arrangement.

These groupings, because of the space requirements, best accommodate from four to six people. There is no doubt that the sofa on the long wall can gather more people about it because a good number of occasional chairs can be focused on the other side of the coffee table. But that should be looked at as a makeshift arrangement suitable for parties only. In the final analysis, your choice of arrangement depends on how you like to entertain and how large your living room is.

The creation of a conversation island is not necessarily confined to the fireplace but may center around a wide window as well. In this

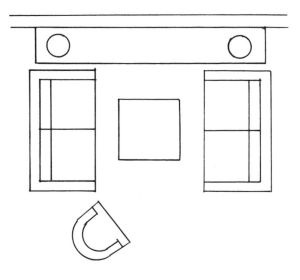

situation, a long, narrow table running alongside the window is effective as a unifying center to the group. If you live in an apartment, it might be advantageous to try placing this arrangement out from the long wall. Here it would be expedient to have a long, narrow table of regular height to give the group a focal point. On this table could be placed lamps of lower than normal height, and behind them on the wall should be a good-looking mirror or painting or even a whole gallery of pictures. It would certainly be a breath of fresh air compared to the usual apartment house arrangement.

This island effect does present a few problems. One of them may be to furnish light for the sectional corner table that is somewhat removed from the fireplace wall. Since wall-to-wall carpeting or large rugs make plug-in lighting inconvenient for the conversation island, we find that with area rugs cords can disappear underneath and happily reappear at the very spot needed for the end table and lamp. If you have problems with cords, remember that we now have many ways to light a room, so it is not necessary for every end table to hold a lamp. It would be a rare family that would need more than three good reading places in one room.

If you have a sofa that is short enough, it might be fun for a change of scenery to try an island arrangement, but it requires a room of the

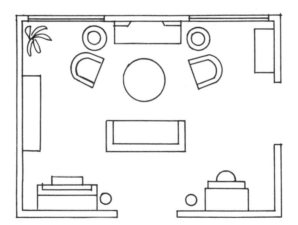

right size and shape. Conversation islands do not look good with corner fireplaces or in rooms that are too small, because you must have enough space not only to fill the empty walls correctly but also to allow good passage in between. You wouldn't want your guests squeezing their way through your furniture.

At first thought it may seem difficult to know what should go against empty walls, but it is really rather simple. All sorts of items— such as desks, secretaries, breakfronts, bookcases, chests, cabinets, stereos, pianos, organs, library tables and console tables—can find a home there, even dad's reading chair. A home owner is lucky indeed if the room is large enough to include still another sofa group, preferably opposite the fireplace.

The fireplace is sometimes ignored as far as arranging furniture is concerned. If openings on both sides of the hearth eliminate the possibility of furniture groupings, a long or short bench or a square ottoman, centered or placed to one side, can be fashionable. Sometimes particularly handsome side chairs can sit on each side with their backs against the chimney breast looking out toward the room. This old French trick is a sure way of supplying extra seating space in a room. And a handsome occasional chair looks smart placed diagonally by the fireplace, particularly if an exquisite screen is placed behind it. Obviously, it is not always necessary to use large upholstered pieces in this focal area, but use something. Don't just let it stand there.

After the sofa, upholstered chairs are the most important pieces of furniture in a living room, but they cannot operate to any degree of comfort without an end table close by, even if the space allows only a tray lamp or small cigarette tables. I have seen comfortable lounge chairs placed in the middle of rooms. Who sits in a chair and does nothing? Only occasional chairs that can easily be picked up and moved according to the whim of the occupant should be given such treatment.

The full-time reading chair, usually with matching ottoman, is at its best when not included with a sofa group. Reading and conversation do not mix. Anyway, an ottoman puts up a good fight with the coffee table and often wins out as the spot where an unthinking person places a coffee cup. Furthermore, it may squeeze space so that the sofa takes a back seat and is difficult to reach.

My favorite reading spot is a corner arrangement having two comfortable chairs face and share the same ottoman or footstool and a large table holding a good reading lamp to fill the corner in between them. It makes an ideal spot for husband and wife togetherness, if the children haven't grabbed it first. The table can be square or round with

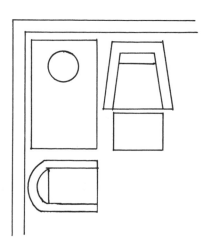

a skirt added for color. If the husband is a bug on being surrounded by tons of reading material, the table can be quite large, thirty by fifty-four inches, with a shelf below. It becomes a great spot with a reading chair and ottoman placed on the long side and my lady's smaller lounge on the short side. This ·can be an excellent arrangement when the wall is somewhat long and there is extra space to be filled.

Be sure your living room doesn't collect too many lounge chairs. After all, how many people need to go the whole way in comfort for the evening in this room? You can give relief by introducing an occasional chair or two.

Effective also is the tremendous diversity shown in tables and in living rooms nowadays. You can select from diminutive cigarette tables, chows or coffee squares, coffee tables, all shapes and sizes of end tables, library tables, console tables, hanging shelves that function as tables, and tray lamps. These practical inventions, all in one piece with center pedestals, answer the need for both a table and a lamp in crowded areas. They have had such success that sometimes they replace end tables.

When a chair is placed diagonally in a corner, a round table is better next to it than a rectangular one because it takes up less room. Using round end tables next to a long sofa that is fronted by an almost equally long coffee table can provide a welcome change of pace. The little cigarette table is at its best when situated neither at the side nor directly in front of its chair, but by the corner so that it is not hard to reach or in the way of passage to the chair. Coffee tables are not placed in front of single chairs for the obvious reason that they are too large.

A coffee table, strategically placed in front of a fireplace with lounge

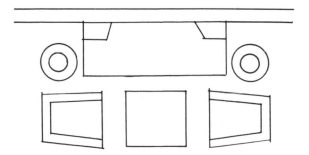

chairs facing it on each side, is superb. At this location it must be square or round and not too large. Please do not allow it to be wider than the chairs facing it. A forty-two-inch, round coffee table may be great between two sofas, but it looks ridiculous between two chairs.

While we are focused on this location, we might as well be aware of the space flanking the fireplace. The old standby here is the built-in bookcase. Not ever a bad idea, but you can't take it with you when you move. The new piece on the market is the bookcase cabinet, which can look distinguished in this location because, although wide, it is narrow in depth and portable. Appropriate also is the small bachelor chest and narrow console table, or even a half-moon shelf bracketed to the wall. All these can hold lamps for reading in the seating spaces arranged at the side of the fireplace.

Now that the sofa is often no longer backed up to the long wall, we find the reappearance of the sofa table or chest to relieve the plainness and heaviness of the sofa back when it is part of a fireplace group. Either one is also a good place for a lamp and reading material.

Although you may be sick and tired of the table in front of the picture window, its popularity substantiates its practicality. Either round or rectangular, it fills space without disturbing the view. It can take a chair on each flank. Just choose lovely pieces to go there with a particularly good-looking lamp and don't worry about it being conventional. It is one of the few arrangements that can achieve balance in rooms having picture windows.

We have long known that no rule prescribes matching tables on each side of the sofa when it is located against a wall. Unmatched tables, however, should be sufficiently different to be interesting. But you might as well not bother with two tables of similar size and shape. In other words, use instead a chest on one side and a rectangular table on the other. Or you might try just one end table, not two. In this case, because of the size of a sofa, the table should be larger than the regular rectangular end table. A square, round or octagonal, open or closed, commode is perfect with a heavy base lamp on it. If more accent color is needed in the room, a round, skirted table can be a stunning addition to your decor. It even looks right with Early American.

When single chests flank the sofa, tables of similar size but lower in height can also be used. If the coffee table is a midget, large end tables are splendid. The lady's writing desk can be put here or it can be placed perpendicular to the wall and sofa.

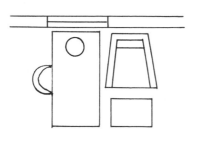

To refresh your memory, a game table and its four semi-upholstered chairs can be flattering additions, if space permits. If, after all this, you are still blessed with too much room, try a large breakfront or at least a secretary against one wall. With a straight back chair on each side of it, it may give your room the symmetry and dignity it needs if you have arranged too asymmetrically. Another judicious use of space is to place a grand piano on the diagonal. It sets an elegant pace without striving to attain it. Lacking space, be smart and follow the lines of the room with the straight side of the piano and have the curved section facing out into the room. Fill the curve of the piano with an upholstered or occasional chair having a curved back, and combine the chair with a round table to create a cozy corner than can also add seating space.

Desks as part of the living room should be located flat against a wall, but with enough space they can be flattering, especially as writing tables jutting out perpendicularly from the wall. The desk serves as table, holding a lamp. A chair, with or without an ottoman can be placed on its long, open side. The arrangement is even better if the wall has a window at that point.

Stereo cabinets under a gallery of paintings settle the problem of what to do with a large empty wall. The family room was invented to house the television, but if the family has divided interests you might avoid arguments by buying a portable for the living room. The fact that it can be wheeled out of the way with ease keeps it from ruining the living room arrangement, as a more expensive console can.

Ottomans and benches for the living room provide extra seating for company, yet are not space grabbers. You can place them where chairs cannot go, skillfully helping to balance a room, and any guest can easily carry them to another location. Inexpensive in comparison with chairs, artistic in design, and correctly placed to add that extra spot of color a room sometimes needs, they are sadly overlooked by most homemakers, who must be simply unaware of where to place them. They neatly fit in front of a stereo, a bookcase, a cabinet, a breakfront, a fireplace, a window, or an empty wall space, particularly on each side of the opening to a room; they can serve as the seat to a secretary or desk, or can be placed on one side of a lady's writing table. It is often smart to use them in pairs.

In visiting various homes, I notice errors in furniture arrangement

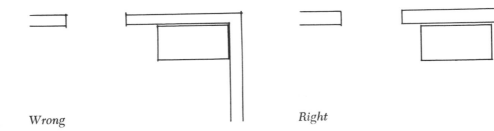

Wrong   *Right*

worth discussing here. I find that the most persistent fault in using wooden furniture lies in shoving a large piece, such as a chest, into a corner when there is plenty of room to spare. Good-looking wood pieces, like worthwhile prints need to be bordered by space in order to be set off. Besides, big pieces balance better if they are centered in a wall space. Another common fault lies in placing all the wooden pieces at one end of the room, making that section appear as cold as an iceberg in January. Instead of that, you should mix the two types of furniture—wood and upholstered—as well as possible. Do not place a desk right next to a spinet piano; relieve the situation by having wooden furniture around either an upholstered piece or a door or window in between.

Always center or balance furniture groups that are opposite each other. Use architectural features in the same way. In planning fireplace arrangments, the shape of the coffee table becomes important. It is all simply a matter of geometry. A narrow, rectangular coffee table simply cannot serve both sides of a fireplace group. If it is made to, the furniture looks too close together; if it doesn't the coffee table looks silly out in the middle. To avoid error, situate your upholstered pieces the correct distance apart in relation to the fireplace opening, then move in with the rectangular coffee table, relating it to one sofa alone. Actually, the rectangular coffee table looks peculiar even with a corner sofa arrangement. Unless the table is unusually wide, the shorter sofa looks ignored. Thus a round, octagonal, or square coffee table works better. Even coffee squares, one for each sofa, can be used effectively.

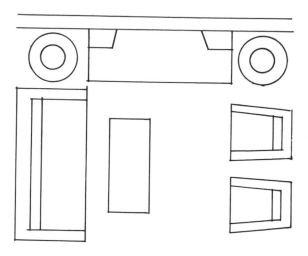

Single bookcases of the movable variety should be centered in their wall spaces. When they are built-in, they should extend in width across the whole wall area. Like the corner fireplace, a room becomes dreadfully off balance when bookcases extend from a corner and end suddenly in the middle of a wall. When located correctly, bookcases are an attractive addition to any room.

Living rooms, particularly those done in Danish Modern, sometimes have a leggy look. Too many bare furniture legs give too much

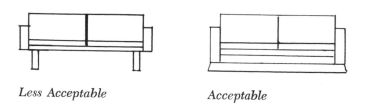

Less Acceptable   *Acceptable*

motion to a room. Check your room for the symptoms. The cure is to buy a piece or two that goes all the way to the floor. With upholstered pieces it is simple. All they need are skirts.

Another fault lies in setting a heavy piece of furniture against a wall of glass that reaches to the floor. It looks dreadful from the patio side and inflicts heaviness where lightness should prevail. For walls of glass, the preference should be chairs without skirts or open tables instead of book commodes. Never place anything like a spinet piano in this location, but a grand piano is a real show-off when near glass.

Coffee tables often do not allow enough walk space in relation to the sofa. It would be ideal if the table could end at least twelve inches in from the sofa arm. This arrangement would allow some leg room with the chair at the sofa's side. A chest in place of a coffee table may be a good conversation piece, but what do you do with your feet? Better under than over, I always say. Even a coffee table with a low shelf finds itself holding up feet and books.

End tables are usually not as long as the chairs they serve—with good reason, too. The chair or sofa is the point of interest, not the table. Just think of the bruises that might occur from miscalculations in

Wrong   *Right*

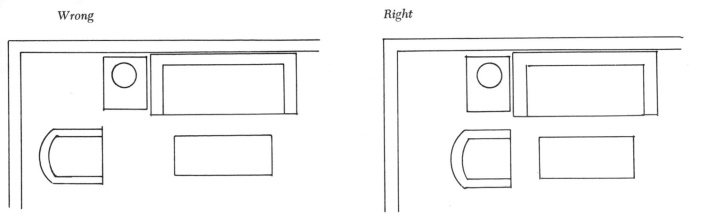

maneuvering into a seat. Should extra space materialize at the front or at the back? An end table can be even with the front of a neighboring upholstered piece or it can be dead center with equal space front and back. The lamp can be centered on the table, but it may be more practical to place it toward the back so that the table itself has more space for other items. I wouldn't place it off center toward the sofa, though, because that ignores the chairs in the group.

Chairs placed on the side of the sofa can take three different positions: straight with the sofa, turned in, and turned out facing the room. Of the three, probably turning the chairs in toward the sofa is the least desirable because then you stare right at the wall. Just don't

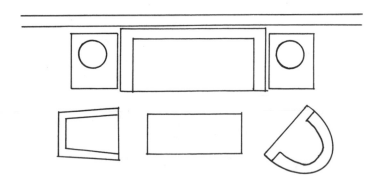

arrange chairs within the seating space of the sofa. The chair seat should end before the sofa arm begins, but if space is at a premium the end of the chair could be moved in as far as the start of the sofa seat. Don't place them so far away from the sofa and end table that they no longer share the end table with the sofa. The usual amount of leftover space from the back of the chair to the wall is no cause for concern; where you sit in relation to the sofa is what matters.

Once in a while, chairs can be placed at the opposite side of the coffee table, facing the sofa. They should never be high back chairs; in this location they tend to divide the room in half, as a screen would. Even heavy lounge chairs look cumbersome out in the middle unless they are part of a conversation island; then they appear right by matching the bulky sofa in a like position. However, you can also choose two small lounge chairs, low back occasional chairs, or a bench for a satisfactory combination.

Start to become critical of furniture arrangements. For instance, when you visit your friends' homes, mentally find fault with what they have done and try to rearrange the room in a better manner. You may be surprised how many practical ideas pop into your head.

We can now step into the dining room. Room arranging here has been much the same for years. The table is in the center of the room. At least four chairs pushed up to the table keep the room from appearing as if it were a doctor's reception room. Six chairs can be used with a big table, but if six chairs are all you have try to fill the empty wall spaces with those two extras. Host and hostess chairs are not so popular now because the arms do not slide easily under the table. When as many as eight are purchased, though, these two are likely to be included in the group.

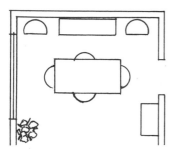

The buffet should be placed against the longest wall. If you have just a dining ell, the longest wall is the only wall against which chairs should be placed and the arrangement should be symmetrical not only because of the huge weight of the buffet in comparison with that of the chair but also because the dining room is the most formal room, and symmetry and formality go together like identical twins. The dining ell can often take another small wooden piece near the kitchen door such as a tiny server, a bachelor's chest, a bar cabinet, or an extra chair with a hanging shelf above for displaying things. The hanging shelf above the chair is legitimate because the chair is not used as a seat in this location.

After World War II, dining rooms as such began to disappear because architects felt they were wasted space that was too costly. The argument has merit if dining rooms are used for just one hour a day. Anyway, the planners eliminated them in preference of the newly conceived family room. I wonder, though, if they realize that in a great many homes the dining room is used more than the living room. Needing space, the smart housewife uses it for dual purposes. If the family is small enough, the table can be relegated to a wall or window; lacking a buffet, the other large piece can be a desk, piano or stereo.

In the early days of television, I had a long banquette built along the window wall and around one corner of my dining room. The dining table pushed up against one end of the lounge, providing seating space at the other end; on the wall opposite the curved side of the built-in sofa sat the television. My family used the room almost the same way as an old-fashioned kitchen, but all the cooking was hidden behind a door.

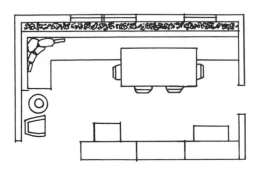
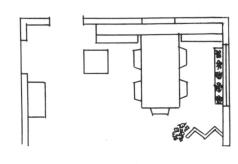

Another time, in a living and dining room combination, the narrow end of the dining table was butted into the center of a wall surrounded by bookcases and cabinets. Nearby, a chest substituted as a buffet. On the left in front of the bookcases was a large, comfortable ottoman. From the living room side, this cozy arrangement appeared to be a library, but since five chairs were seated around the table there was no problem converting it at night into the eating area.

As a bride, I moved to a Florida town near an air base during World War II. Many of the newlyweds like me were lucky enough to live in little honeymoon cottages, all furnished exactly the same but architecturally interesting with their attractive tiled floors and two wide windows with glass to the floor. Filling the floor in the window areas with many exotic potted plants, covering the round dining table with a skirt of apricot chintz, and setting an equally inexpensive all white lamp on the table along with books and a few wedding gifts, I created a chic lived-in look that the other cottages lacked. The table top had to be cleared for meals, but I had plenty of time in those days to do that simple task.

Later, I moved to an old house in which the living room was rather dark and the dining room large and cheery. I placed the table against a wall and at the other end of the room had bookcases built on each side of a large window. In the window was placed the family kneehole desk; overstuffed Victorian lounge chairs, covered in gay slip covers, were located on each side of the desk. In the daytime these chairs seated the family, who moved into the living room as darkness fell.

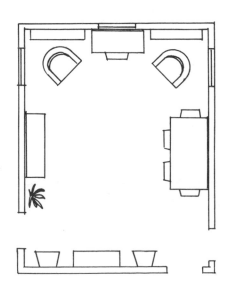

In Charlottesville, Virginia, I worked with another dining room with folding doors; the far end of the room was enlarged by a rectangular bay window. Grandmother visited several months out of the year and this room became hers. A hide-a-bed and end tables were placed in the bay. Small occasional chairs and a small coffee square flanked the group. French closets were built on each side. One opened as a clothes closet; the other had drawers for linen storage. The room was large enough to accommodate the centered dining table even when the hide-a-bed was opened. The dining room is great for more than eating if you are short of space.

Even so, using the dining room in a dual role is considered a handicap by most women. A separate dining room, according to real estate reports, is high on the list of requirements for the American housewife, and she undoubtedly wishes to use it only for dining. If the dining room is large, you must use more furniture.

The main problem with dining room furniture is the coldness it conveys because of so much exposed wood. Thus the use of color and pattern whenever feasible is smart on your part. It is a great place for the display of carefully chosen bric-a-brac. But please do not install those overcrowded, glass china cabinets from the thirties. They always jangled when you walked by them. Plants can soften the room, and if the room is large enough a bird cage far from the table can extend a cheery note. If wallpaper is not preferred, bare walls are ideal for vivid paintings.

I have noticed a couple of problems almost universal in dining room arrangements. The expected formality of the room is lost when the well-meaning housewife places the dining chairs on the diagonal in a corner. This error probably occurs from unconsciously sensing that the room is too stark. It spoils the lines of the room and hides the attractive designs on the backs of the side chairs which show up better when placed directly against the wall. Only in very informal or squeezed circumstances would this arrangement be acceptable.

Contractors rarely hang the chandelier in the right spot. Although I usually avoid advising the swag chain (resembling a ship's rigging) that constantly shows up on hanging lamps, at times it may help to solve the problem of the off-centered chandelier. In a dual purpose dining room, the table may be centered one place for the family and another place for dinner parties. Two hooks in the ceiling and an extra long chain can provide a simple solution to the tricky problem. Adjust the height of the chandelier properly. Three feet from the bottom of the chandelier to the table top is a good allowance.

Bedrooms are more complicated than dining rooms because age and the number of occupants are pertinent to the arrangement. As for the master bedroom be sure when you purchase the house that all your bedroom furniture can fit in it. Builders sometimes do not allow enough room for a king-size bed, two night stands and the other wooden pieces.

Naturally, such a large affair as the master bed should be centered with the headboard against a wall so that no one has to climb over anyone else to get into or out of bed. Then, too, since bedtime is favored for reading, both husband and wife need good lighting and a place to put down their reading material when Morpheus insists on taking over.

Probably the most attractive position for the bed is the one in which it can be viewed head-on as you enter the room; little is lost, though, if this arrangement cannot be achieved. Just don't forget

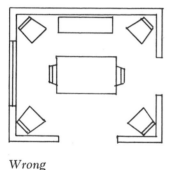

Wrong

that the bed is the center of interest in a bedroom and so deserves extra attention. An especially handsome headboard can perk up a monotonous bedroom. Four-posters are now back in style. If that man of yours lets you get away with it, buy a canopy of any type for your new four-poster bed. It's a sure-to-succeed item. And buy the best bedspread you can afford. Always a treat for the eye, it aids tremendously in relieving dullness. Today's heavy bedspreads take so long to wear out that they cannot help being economical. You can never go wrong by covering a plywood headboard with the same fabric as the bedspread. In a ranch house, the master bedroom

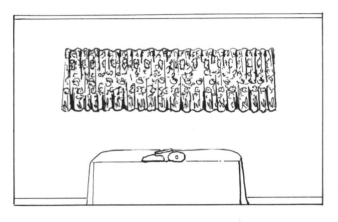

Wrong

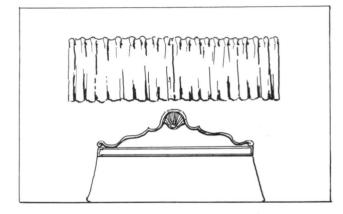

Right

often suffers because of a wide window high above the bed. If that is your problem, minimize the excessive wall space by using a high headboard.

A king-size bed is gigantic, but its wide expanse can be visually reduced by using a printed bedspread. If a plain bedspread is preferred, use decorator pillows to break the appearance of the bed's width. Unless your bedroom is large, think twice before you purchase a king-size bed. The queen-size is a better decorating choice and most couples find its width sufficient for comfort.

The matched bedroom groups that now flood the market—ranging from pseudo Spanish Renaissance to Modern—should be guardedly considered unless they are made by the best name furniture companies. The pieces lack the delight of surprise. How much more character and spontaneity are exhibited by bedrooms whose pieces were bought one at a time or even contain hand-me-downs. Although frilly dressing tables are of slight use because we have extensive makeup areas in bathrooms, one nevertheless lends a change of pace to bedroom furniture. Additionally, a fully upholstered chair with a skirt and perhaps a pretty, skirted round table helps eschew that antiseptic look.

Tables or chests beside the bed need not match the set or each other. At one time I had long benches on the sides of our low bed, and the effect was great. Think what a well-planned night table might hold:

lamp, telephone, ash tray, clock, radio, electric blanket control, space for books and magazines, room for snack dishes, and anything else to make this a favorite relaxation center. As you can readily see, the usual night stand is woefully inadequate.

Chests and bureaus are best near the closet and bath areas, but we cannot stand them in a row unless they are designed to take such a position. The amount of wall space available must therefore be taken into consideration, with the triple dresser donated to the largest space. Ask yourself if you really need a triple dresser. The room is probably filled by the king-size bed anyway.

Even though you may not wish to set up your bedroom as a second sitting room, I hope you have room for a comfortable chair. After all, the master bedroom is your private sanctum. If the space does not warrant the chair as a separate unit with its own table, the night table can be a good substitute. Since corners are often the only unused space in bedrooms, chairs with curved backs and round tables are good choices here. The end table would naturally be on the opposite side of the chair from the night stand. Benches at the end of the bed can be most helpful, particularly if you fold down your bedspread at night or need space for laying clothes out. A side chair, even that extra one from the dining room, may be the perfect answer for your bedroom's small, extra space.

It is amazing to see how the bedroom is turning into a dual purpose room today. When family togetherness gets to us during the loud, lively teenage period, many a parent turns to the quiet solace of his bedroom for safety. If the den has had to be released to a

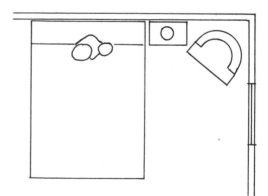

child for a private bedroom of his own, the master bedroom may find itself harboring the desk. Mother may well wish to sit in a comfortable chair beside it as dad struggles with his homework from the office. We may even go further with a whole little sitting group consisting of love seat and chairs, built-in bookcases, and the second television. This agreeable arrangement may even be accomplished in the smaller room if you give up your king-size bed and triple dresser for a queen and armoire.

Children's rooms are another story, and girls' rooms have different requirements from boys'. Every child should have as much floor space as is manageable. It doesn't bother me that a bed pushed into a corner against a wall is hard to make. A child doesn't make a good bed no matter where it is. The most floor space for girls can be had by using opposite corners for beds. Even though only one child is to use the bedroom, two beds are always good because from a certain age almost to the time they are married girls love to share their room on weekends with an overnight guest, or two, or three, or four. Floor space is needed to make room for bed rolls. The daughter's own room is much preferred for all this activity.

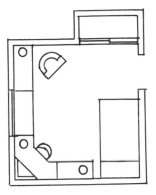

A girl needs much more drawer space than a boy. Remember all those sweaters you had as a teenager? Buy plenty of chests. In today's small rooms, matched groups that line the walls with chests, desks, bookcases, commodes and the like may be tiresome, but they are practical. The funny thing, though, is that it is a rare girl who uses her desk after the age of fourteen. Instead, she heads for the bed for studying. It may be that years of bending over books in this awkward position is one cause of all the backache problems. The desk is great for piles of books. So is the dressing table. What a girl needs is a whole bathroom to herself, not a dressing table.

A full-length mirror is an asset to a girl's room if the bathroom doesn't have one. There should be one deep wooden piece to hold a portable record player. Next to the bed should be lighting that can be easily turned off from the bed. A radio for bedtime listening should also be close at hand. Shelves are necessary for doll or toy or hobby collections. And give your girl a big bulletin board for a messy display of her social life.

The comfortable chair will not be used for sitting, but it is the best answer for stacking all the clothes she has been trying on since she got up yesterday. She may share her bed with millions of soft, furry animals, and there may not be a clear space in the whole room. It may be messy, but oh does it have the lived-in look! Do not despair. She will marry and come back home one day to criticize your sloppy housekeeping.

Your daughter is usually a victim of fads and dearly loves to have an exact replica of her favorite girl friend's room. They run color schemes as if there were no tomorrow and are generally feminine in their desire for pastels. Most of them pick out traditional furniture in the particular style of the moment, and they adore anything as soft and fluffy as the animals they collect. Since they do not play with mechanical toys or with games on the floor as much as their brothers, a fluffy area rug thrills them to death. They delight in the feel of things and unconsciously seek out ruffles and bows, even though they may swing a mean bat and be caught climbing trees on their lonely days. If there is room for a large, low ottoman, they and their friends may enjoy flip-flopping all over it.

Canopies in a girl's room can be cute as a button, but think carefully before you purchase one. Two single full-fledged canopies may

make a room look as if white puffy clouds were settling. If a room is too small, even a single one can be overpowering. However, if a bedroom is large, a double bed with a canopy can be the envy of the younger set for miles around. Canopies are somewhat ineffective when the bed snuggles up to the side walls. If the room is big enough, purchase a canopy and place it in the old-fashioned way in the middle of the room. Today's girl is definitely seeking the shut-in feeling in interior decorations, and a canopy answers this purpose.

Of course, a full canopy is not the only possibility. You can settle for a half-canopy for the twin beds; fabric forms a ruffle high above the bed and should cover the bed as far as the pillow does underneath. This arrangement can also have draperies at the headboard and side. For another effect, the fabric can come swagging up, looping through a ring high above the headboard to come down again on the other side. This style is equally smart if the bed is centered with the long side against the long wall like a French daybed. The fabric comes up over matching footboard and headboard to a crown in the center. A bracket extending from the wall holds the crown.

If on those weekends your daughter and her girlfriends prefer bed rolls to beds, a single bed in the room is sufficient. With the length of the bed against the wall and with bolsters at the backside and perhaps also at the foot and headboard, a very up-to-date daybed effect can be achieved. The only trouble is where to put those bolsters from bedtime until morning. A carpenter or a handy husband can build closets or bookshelves on each side of the bed to create a cozy nook in the French manner.

As you know, little boys are made of something different. You'll have to make some ingenious hideaway plan for the rarely used train set or race track. Outside of suggesting a completely separate room, like the garage, I almost give up. Young boys want their toys at their fingertips and do a great deal of playing on the floor, so their rooms should have plenty of floor space. The beds around the corner with a corner table are perfect.

For the type of floor playing that goes on, low pile rugs should be used. I get so irked with mothers who insist on deep piled area rugs for their boy's room. Boys usually do not prefer the bed for studying. They may even use the desk for that purpose, although the floor sometimes is chosen. Besides a desk, your boy needs lots of shelves, not only for books but also to display the creations of his hobbies. His interests are status symbols which must not be hidden in a closet. He is very fond of posters, reproductions of art, or his own dabblings. He likes a bulletin board, too, which he will be neater about than his sister. And give him space for the record player and a place for his radio near the bed.

He does not need as much drawer space as a girl does, and he actually uses his comfortable chair for an occasional bout with the books. A mirror over his tall chest would probably please him immensely because he is discovering himself. He prefers rich, dark colors with contemporary furniture. You may find a good chest, a large desk (perhaps going across a whole wall), a comfortable chair and lots of bookcases and shelves all he will need. So don't bother trying to use up all available wall space with matching pieces that fit together in a row.

Above all, try to make your boy's room workable for him. I think it is a fine way of making him happy enough to stay home once in a while as he reaches the teenage period, as well as to create a pleasant place to rendezvous with his friends.

I remember one ten-year-old boy's room that was decorated to the hilt. The room deserved a gold star for smartness and originality, but zero for livability. Twin beds came out from the wall in the center of the room and took up almost all the floor space. The bedspreads, machine quilted by his mother, portrayed a wharf scene of early Virginia. Since she was a would-be artist, his mother painted on the wall behind the beds greatly enlarged duplicates of the figures printed on the spreads, all arranged around the headboards. But the beds could not be relocated because of the painted area. The night stand in between was a brightly painted barrel. A bench, an old pirate chest, and a chest of drawers completed the room. When I dared to ask where the boy was going to play and study in his room, I was told she did not believe in using bedrooms for anything but sleeping. The boy was to use the family room for these other purposes. The bedroom was not the boy's, but his mother's to show off to her friends.

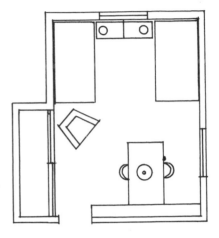

Although fewer faults are to be found in arranging bedrooms than living rooms, some occasionally occur. The worst is to shove a chest of drawers smack into a corner with no room to spare. Remember, center big wooden pieces in wall spaces whenever possible.

Another fault is that anything as large as a double bed looks like a ghost with its head cut off it if it does not have a headboard. Perhaps if your budget doesn't allow a good one for a while, a little ingenuity can whip up an inexpensive one, even if it has to be painted on the wall behind. There is always the old gate picked up for a song at the local junk yard; or the sagging lattice at the end of the garden, straightened, painted and newly framed; or the shaped piece of plywood cut in your husband's tool shop and upholstered in a fabric quilted by your machine; or Japanese matting tacked to a straight plywood headboard with a simple trim nailed on to cover the raw edges; or a needlepoint covered headboard; or a homemade frame holding woven rope taut; or an elaborate paneled door from an old house. I am sure you will have no trouble coming up with something unusual once you put your mind to it.

I do have objections, however, to the bookcase headboard in a traditional atmosphere. It becomes a place for clutter, a catchall for the books the husband and wife have finished reading, rather than for new ones they plan to start. You can only read one book at a time, the top of the bookcase is too narrow to hold much of anything, and all but lean-over lamps look bad on it.

Another poor idea is the hanging lamp over the middle of the bed. I have heard of people rising suddenly in the middle of the night and almost knocking themselves out on the monstrous things. Far better to keep these objects, never my favorites, hanging over the night stand. If you feel that you just do not have enough room on your night stand and must have hanging lamps, be sure they have shades and give good light for reading.

In the family room, the main purpose is viewing, not conversation. We do not need short sofas surrounded by lounge chairs. The conversation island fails utterly. What we need is a long wall that can harbor the nine-foot sofa or longer affairs that just a short time ago were the darlings of the living room. Then there will be plenty of room for everyone to see the tube across the room. If a couple of characters wish to lie down with the comfort of a Roman at leisure, they may do so with room to spare.

Leave a large empty space in the middle of the room for children's games, for the grown or almost grown male who feels more at ease when stretched out on the floor, and for teenage dancing. The walls of the family room are great for bulletin boards to take care of those art masterpieces that keep coming home during the elementary school years. Try housing the ironing board here, too. The pull-down ironing board of the 1930s, transferred from the kitchen to the family room, can solve your storage problem and can make snatch ironing no fuss at all. If closets with folding doors are built in the family room, a perfect little sewing center can be fashioned to disappear behind the doors when not in use. Open shelves, both high and low, can handle all the toys. The small family may even wish to go Scandinavian and have in front of the sofa a long eating table that can be used for quiet games while others watch television.

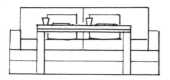

The family room should be geared for rough activity. In the living room, children should learn to act like little ladies and gentlemen, but it would be a mean mother who would squelch animal spirits in the family room. The tile floor appears to be a better answer than wood, and the wood is a better answer than wall-to-wall carpet. Spills are bound to occur. An area rug of low pile, perhaps a tweed, would be practical for the family room. Tile, unlike wood, does not call for a full carpeting. Children can play with ease on a low pile, and a tweed or pattern helps hide dirt and spots.

For a lively family, a plastic such as Naugahyde may be the answer for furniture coverings. It takes a destructive child with an ice pick to damage it, and there are not too many of those around anymore— ice picks, I mean. Plastic may not last seven years if used constantly, but it is a reasonable buy in comparison with woven fabrics. There is not much that you cannot scrub off it. Unfortunately, as it ages it tends to tear next to the welt. Comfortable, inexpensive pillows can easily be replenished as they become dirty and beat up with constant use.

Lamps should be fat and sturdy in this active room and should be placed on solid tables. Since it is the play area, indirect lighting is good here, and table lamps should be placed away from traffic.

No matter how you decide to furnish it, think of this room as a variety room: a play room, a work room, a movie room, an eating room, and even a guest room.

And now the hall. Whatever happened to that grand entrance hall that ran from one end of the house to the other in which a big table stood for thrown school books, a chair for coats, and another chair for sitting down to put on overshoes when it snowed, an umbrella stand, a pedestal for a Boston fern, and a mirror for that last minute glance? Ah, that was a hall! Today we barely take one step in, and we are out of it. No wonder it is so plain and uninteresting.

At least get some wallpaper on the wall and a smart area rug on the floor. Make the door rug pretty. Small fringed rugs of the same pattern as the living room carpet can be placed in the strategic spots along the hall. You ladies who feel that wall to wall carpeting in your hall is a waste of good money might try this idea instead of the popular ceramic tile that presently heads the list in the contractor's book. Ceramic tile looks bare and cold, but its main fault is that it breaks up the sense of flow that floors particularly need in small or average houses. Any kind of tile is better than composition flooring here. Only vinyl patterns of brick or slate are successful enough to be used in the entrance hall.

Have you ladies forgotten what a great place a hall is for a mirror with a handsome frame? It increases the size of your entrance and hangs so nicely on wallpaper. If wallpaper is not for you, brighten the walls with pictures and decorate a corner with a plant. If your hall is big enough, use a bench with a gayly upholstered seat. The small curio cabinet is also popular. The same shape, but costlier, is the grandfather's clock, always a stately offering for a guest's eye. Hanging shelves or console tables can substitute for the popular chest. You can even have fun with a humorous, old-fashioned coat-rack. But whatever you do, get some color in there to liven up your entrance hall. You know how important first impressions are.

The next chapter is designed to bring you closer to the realities of buying so that you understand how to coordinate in good taste the commodities found on the market and how to avoid the pitfalls that advertising never mentions and sometimes produces.

౭ **6**

Helpful Buying Hints

A pleasing effect comes from the controlled mixture of various furniture styles, but many people are confused about how to properly create such a mixture. Periods may even be mixed to a degree. Furniture periods can be characterized as formal and informal, or perhaps it would be more descriptive to say feminine and masculine. For example, if the designs of the periods being considered are light and delicate in feeling, or somewhat heavy but with an elaborate overuse of the curve, they would tend to enjoy each other's company. If, on

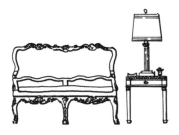

Formal   *Informal*

the other hand, they are permeated by a feeling of strength and bulkiness, whether ornate or simple, the pieces would look well together. As we glance backward through time, we usually see the early development of civilization in a country producing furniture somewhat masculine in feeling; conversely, when a high degree of culture is reached, the design often turns more feminine in its creation. Another factor to remember about style is that the physical characteristics of a people reflect a mood in their furniture. The Spanish are very masculine, and their furniture never leaves this quality far behind. The French are more refined looking, and their furniture is, except at the time it was under the domination of Napoleon, light and gay in proportions. The honest simplicity of the Danes is reflected in their famous "Danish Modern" that ignores applied design.

Some period furnishings that go well together are Louis XV and XVI, English eighteenth-century and Regency, American Federal and our refined dressy modern. Along with these we could include any scaled-down-to-size pieces from the Italian Baroque and Louis XIV periods.

Informal styles include early Italian Renaissance, Spanish Renaissance, English up to Queen Anne, Early American, turn of the century Mission, bulky Modern, and the designs now coming out of Denmark.

Some periods blend with any type of furniture, depending on the

Louis XVI

American Federal

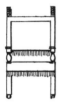

Italian Renaissance

Early American

Queen Anne

French Provincial

choice of upholstery fabrics. These "either way" periods include Queen Anne, French Provincial, most French Empire, American Empire, Victorian, Oriental, and the ever-popular Italian Provincial. Early Danish Modern is certainly informal, but it is not bulky so it does not go well with, say, Spanish Renaissance, but Early American of Shaker simplicity looks good with it.

There were once many more wooden than upholstered pieces in evidence in a home. Because upholstered furniture was used more and, in wearing out sooner, was much more likely to be discarded by the homeowner, few upholstered pieces from the past still exist. As a matter of practicality, I would question the desirability of owning any of these old designs because most do not suit our present casual manner of sitting. It is therefore logical that some of our most beautiful rooms combine simple, straight lined, bulky, and modern upholstered pieces with the old-worldliness of wooden furniture and occasional antique chairs. The room is comfortable, yet has the variety, interest, and perhaps warmth that antiques can add to a room. A sleek, metal, glass-topped coffee table, particularly if area rugs are part of the decor, can accentuate the antiques in a room.

Buy *copies* of antiques if you cannot afford the real thing. Some

Early American

Duncan Phyfe

lucky Americans live with their furniture heritage: New England is still loaded with Early American furniture and later types, including Duncan Phyfe's Federal styles; the Hudson River Valley preserves some heavy ornate Dutch pieces; from Philadelphia to Charleston, handsome Colonial eighteenth-century reigns, with a touch here and there of American Federal; the French left their mark on New Orleans; the Mississippi Valley bears up under an overdose of Victorian, as does San Francisco; and in some sections of the Southwest and southern California traces of early Spanish furniture can be found. These styles are our heritage.

Two popular styles being reproduced are French Provincial and the English eighteenth-century furniture of Queen Anne, Chippendale,

Dutch Renaissance

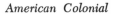

American Colonial

Louis XV

Victorian

Spanish Renaissance

Adam, Hepplewhite, and Sheraton. Early American furniture is inexpensive enough to have found vast popularity. Stark simplicity is its keynote. Good reproductions of authentic Early American are, of course, expensive.

Authentic upholstered pieces are rare because our ancestors owned few other than wing chairs. One false idea is the use of a wing on a sofa. The wing was invented to protect bare necks and bald heads from the cold drafts so common in early houses. The need for the wing went with the draft, but traditional design demands a wing chair just as a traditional room requires a fireplace though it is no longer used for cooking and heating. A wing on a sofa is bad taste; it is a purposeless transfer. Far better, if you hanker for that "Early" look, to pick simple designed upholstered pieces from the next period up the line, the Colonial Period, and settle for such fine designs as the Chippendale sofa, the Martha Washington chair, and the wing chair. The unpretentious Lawson sofa and lounge chair would work out well, too.

Italian Provincial furniture has a misleading name if ever there was one. It is the creation of United States designers who needed to fill a void in home furnishings—it is a refined style without being ostentatious. It was inspired by a combination of styles: Louis XVI, French Directoire (the period in France after the Revolution and before Napoleon), French Empire and even English Regency. Practically all of it on the market is in good taste and has been well received.

Italian Provincial

The least expensive furniture is modern, then Early American, and close behind is some Italian Provincial. We all know that we get what we pay for, so I advise spending as much for your furniture as you can lay your hands on—particularly for upholstered pieces because your comfort is at stake and because upholstery must stand up under the strain of family use. It costs so much to reupholster today that it is cheaper to invest in good construction and long-wearing fabrics.

Although you cannot rip a chair apart to see the inside construction, you can rely to a degree on advertised brands, nationally and sectionally. Established firms have a reputation to uphold, so they cannot afford to have a female gossip campaign of complaints against them. And as far as wear is concerned, heavy, closely woven fabrics last longest. Multicolored fabrics, from mixed tweeds to woven patterns such as tapestries and matelasses, offer you the most freedom from worry. Plain pastels invite dirt and spots, but there are rooms that look so beautiful in light colors that they deserve all the extra care they require. *Scotch Guard* or the other silicone finishes *Syl-mer* and *Zepel* are a help, but they certainly are not the answer to a lazy housewife's prayer. Care still must be the rule of procedure. Any purchase of an upholstered piece should include arm covers, and for the deep or high back lounge chair a back piece for the head is necessary to guard against hair oils. Like a Greek statue, the arms are the first to go, so covers are money in the bank for you. If you feel they resemble the skin on a hippopotamus, as I do, don't use them until your furniture has aged and the arms are beginning to fray. Separate back cushions spell comfort, and like the seat cushions they can be turned over when dirt or wear becomes excessive.

Enticing though they may be, beware of the new all-upholstered pieces with the cut out arms. And I do mean all-upholstered—from top down to the last inch on their little legs. Although they are style setters, their designers must be in cahoots with upholsterers. Their arms and legs readily show wear and smudges, and I hesitate even to estimate the cost of a reupholstering job.

There are many types of fibers on the market and many more are coming. Although natural fibers are generally prettier and longer lasting than synthetics, they are also generally more expensive. Cotton makes the best fabric in the upholstery line, but it is not particularly dressy. Rayon, a very adaptable synthetic, can look dressy and, if heavy, also wears well. For one reason or another, different fibers are combined and cotton and rayon are considered to make a perfect alliance. Linen, nature's most handsome informal fiber, lasts five thousand years on a mummy and can hang for decades at a window, but it shows its weakness when bent at a sofa's edge or made into a welt for the seam. It also does not take dye as well as most other fibers, and once in a great while it does an outlandish thing—with constant friction, the pattern simply rubs off, disappearing into thin air. Still, none of these factors is bad enough to stop me from using linen. My living room it full of it. If you are afraid of it, buy fabrics made of linen and cotton. The beauty is almost all there, plus longer wearing quality. Wool, like linen, is an attractive fiber. Its colors are rich and full of depth, it wears well, but it is even more expensive. Wool and Danish Modern are both informal enough to go together, and wool is also compatible with Early American. Both styles have their roots in the north country.

Silk catches the beauty of color as no other fabric can, but you must pay for this spectacle. Our most expensive fiber and our dressiest, it unfortunately does not give us our money's worth in wear. Silk also can be woven in conjunction with other fibers and naturally its tensile strength improves when it is.

More varieties of synthetics are found in drapery fabrics than in upholstery fabrics. Those used for sitting purposes, besides rayon, are generally woven in conjunction with other fibers for heavy wear. Just don't go overboard for some new fabric that has risen suddenly on the scene. Tried and tested in the lab does not mean tried and tested in the home. There are plenty of good reliables around waiting for your choice.

Besides cotton, rayon, spun rayon, linen, wool, mohair, jute, and silk for upholstery fabrics, nylon is somewhat popular. Esthetically not the most beautiful of fibers, it is strong; although it is sometimes used in a hundred percent strength, it is favored when combined with from one to three other fibers. Notice that acetate (a weak fiber, but reasonable in price) is introduced only in conjunction with others.

Leather has no substitute. You know the smell of real leather. Unlike plastic, leather can be used for both formal and informal situations. In a pastel or bright color, leather is smart on traditional French chairs, even when they are painted white. Suede, leather's reverse side, looks good with Spanish and contemporary furniture, but if you own a pair of suede shoes you know that it doesn't take kindly to rough usage. Stains show up on it, too. And don't go along under the misconception that leather lasts forever.

I am partial to prints, but they call for relatively lightweight material. But if practicality is a requirement, slip covers will please you more than upholstery. If the print is quilted, the price of the fabric is considerably higher, but under this treatment the material becomes as long wearing as any upholstery fabric. Since the casual lived-in look is back, we find the tide of dislike for slipcovers turning. They need not fit like a glove, and the cleaning proposition is *so* simplified. If they are preshrunk, you can take care of the washing yourself. If not, using coin-op dry cleaning machines won't put you in the poor house.

Printing is most effective on cotton and linen. Printed synthetics generally aren't so attractive. Heavy cotton prints wear longer, but linen prints are more handsome and, according to the type of print, can almost upstage themselves in a dressy part. Naturally, slipcovers need not be a print; plain fabrics do nicely. Skirts are part of the appeal of slipcovers, so for a change try ruffled ones for an informal, traditional interior.

Crisp and delightful, chintz, a glazed cotton, can add up to sheer delight as a slipcover or upholstery fabric. Its slight sheen can put it in the formal class, far above its plain, unglazed sister. According to its pattern it is suitable for the formal living room, the master bedroom, daughter's bedroom, or in the kitchen for seat covers and draperies. I must report, though, that chintz does not keep its glaze through repeated cleanings, although it is far from ruined by them. Still, its shiny surface tends to keep it cleaner than its more popular substitute, Glosheen. And the price is right for any size pocketbook.

It goes without saying that shiny fabrics with delicate designs are dressy, while dull, heavy plied fabrics with massive crude patterns tend to be informal. Velvet alone is both, tending to be masculine in heavy colors and feminine in pastel. The more antiqued the texture, the better it blends with informal furniture. Corduroy, a country cousin of velvet, is trying hard to take on city ways, but will never make it.

Loads of exquisite fabrics are not found by the yard in department stores or even in sample books at the local upholsterer. Decorators have these available at their finger tips. Let them help you choose your upholstery or slipcover fabrics. I know you will be delighted to see how many beautiful fabrics there are in this world.

Now that we know where to find them, how do we use them in the room? Today, it is popular to cover the sofa with a pattern and spread the colors taken from the pattern throughout the room. This technique does not necessarily mean that the rest of the room should try to compete with a rainbow. By no means should every color in the pattern be repeated in the room. If a pattern shows more than two colors, there is no need really to bring out more than the two dominant ones, with a touch of the others in accessories here and there if you wish. Or you may upholster or cover all your large pieces alike, reserving the plain fabrics or self-toned patterns for your occasional chairs, side chairs, and benches. If the contemporary style pleases you most, plain fabrics on all of your pieces fill the bill, keeping the number of colors down to three. It is well to remember, too, that large plaids have a way of being knockouts when placed on bulky modern sofas.

It would be best, of course, to upholster matching chairs alike, even though in your present home they may not be placed in matching positions. Plaids or stripes mix admirably with printed fabric. I cannot imagine where the rumor started that this conglomerate is incorrect. Stripes should be somewhat proportionate to the size of the

Acceptable

Less Acceptable

furniture on which they are placed. Wide stripes suit large pieces, and pin stripes are proper on chair seats. Stripes generally look best running vertically. Horizontal stripes look right to me only when, on a bulky modern sofa, they are wide and subtle in coloring. Two different colored fabrics on one chair is not fashionable. Did you really like two-toned automobiles? It looks even worse on furniture. It is only feasible on a French bergere, on which the back can be done in plain velvet or satin to match one of the colors used in the brocade on the front.

If your windows are not too wide, the draperies can be a print, and perhaps one or more pieces of furniture, such as a wing chair opposite, can repeat the print. If the carpet has a pattern, you may prefer all the furniture to be covered in plain fabrics, or in self-patterned damasks, but it is not absolutely necessary. If planned this way, though, the decorator pillows should be in distinctive prints. Believe it or not, small sitting rooms can exhibit a unified and delightful effect with all the upholstered pieces and draperies done in the same print. But a large room would look ridiculous decorated in that manner.

As far as wooden pieces are concerned, careful buying, even hampered by a slim purse, can find good designs. Budgeting is especially possible in contemporary designs, which explains their popularity among the young married group. But it is always true that the more inexpensive the furniture is the cheaper the wood, and the more necessary it becomes to cover large surfaces with Formica or high gloss finishes, to be limited to rough interiors in the drawers, and perhaps to add extraneous designs to cover up poor wood and poor workmanship. The more you spend on wooden furniture, the handsomer the wood, the lovelier the finishes, the better the moving parts.

If modern furniture does not appeal to you and you wish to become knowledgeable in reproductions, carefully study the originals by reading up on antiques. Second, subscribe to the top decorating magazines (you can recognize them because they are the highest priced ones on the market).

You may consider that the rooms shown (when viewed as a whole) are too high style for you, but that is not the point. You are interested in the furniture, so concentrate on it alone. Handsome pieces make up these rooms. If you can, find out what company manufactures them. Absolutely free, or for a few dollars, you can send away for brochures on these fine pieces.

Lucky you if you can afford the tops in these reproductions; if you cannot, at least your eye will have been trained to buy the best for less. Remember to avoid the uneasy diagonal line for furniture legs unless it copies the old saw horse pattern. Be sure that any applied design strengthens the structure of the piece you are buying and that the ornamentation is not excess baggage. The basic design of furniture (or, for that matter, any decorative creation) should never be so covered that the basic shape of the structure is lost. And do not show your ignorance by insisting on "solid" pieces. Furniture legs on most pieces must be solid, but chest fronts and table tops are subject to the use of veneer, particularly when manufactured in top quality wood. Exquisite grain patterns show up especially in walnut, mahogany, rosewood and fruitwood. Solid pieces are for the common woods—oak, maple, pine and birch—used so much for informal styles.

You can add a piece or two of painted furniture to your potpourri. If the room is primarily traditional, the piece may feel more at home if it is antiqued. Pick out a color that adds to your scheme. Your choice for this piece should be a significant one, such as a chest, desk or a "conversation piece" coffee table. The resurgence of high gloss painted furniture has taken place lately. This shining effect is always smart for the unmatched piece you have introduced into a room, but it can even be captivating on traditional pieces such as the dining room table, a console table or a secretary. Think about it if you have a piece to refinish. The results of home antiquing kits are getting a little tiresome.

Man has done wonders with some of nature's fibers and woods, developing them into the interesting materials of cane, wicker, bentwood and rattan. Cane for chair seats and backs looks right anytime, anywhere. Wicker, the humorous imp of the furniture world, has fun with Victorian (the period in which it came into this world), Early American, Mission, Danish Modern, Oriental and Modern. It has even popped up into the Spanish decorative arts field. Bentwood chairs, the darlings of the early ice cream parlors, are informal and look good either natural or brightly painted. They go well with the same periods as wicker. Rattan, of Eastern origin, can have an elegance worthy of the most formal interiors. Unfortunately, there are more monstrosities in this line than in any other furniture ever

Cane-back Chair   *Wicker Chair*   *Bentwood Chair*   *Rattan Chair*

designed, and top designing usually demands top price. Keep in mind your principles of art when purchasing anything of this species. Whole rooms of it are tiring, but some pieces, including upholstered furniture, are superb in a modern room (I am talking about the living room in addition to the sun porch and family room). I particularly like rattan with some elaborately carved Chinese teakwood pieces. The effect can be extremely appealing. From the seventeenth century on, Oriental objets d'art and rugs found their way into the homes of France, England and America; as a result, the traditional decor can include some Eastern accessories. A simple piece of rattan fits in well with them and adds to the delicacy of the Oriental influence.

Great sums need not be spent on your drapery fabric. For the sunny side of the house, you may wish to invest in material that has a guarantee. You might notice, though, that the guarantee is for fading, not rotting, and that the fabrics guaranteed are usually man-made, not natural fibers. The truth of the matter is that, generally, synthetics fade less but rot sooner than natural fibers. The perfect fiber has yet to be invented. So we often find in drapery and curtain fabrics a mixture of fibers, sometimes as many as five. One might be inexpensive to help keep the price down. Another might be outstanding in its color fastness. Perhaps another is noted for being impervious to rotting, but by itself would exhibit other serious problems. Still another may not change with the climate. The least used may be one of nature's fibers, included for beauty's sake.

In informal fabrics, as far as sun is concerned, cotton is not a bad buy. After all, what is drapery lining but cotton? The fact that draperies aren't backed with a synthetic ought to tell us something that is not even implied in advertisements. Cotton is slow to rot, and the dyes are fairly good today except in the strongest colors. Lining protects against fading, and I would line all printed and highly colored draperies because they simply look terrible from outside the house. White or off-white draperies need not be lined.

Many fabulous casement cloths are on the market today. A casement cloth with its see-through quality doesn't have to be lined; in fact, the interesting texture is lost if the play of light is blocked off. You can of course fix up two traverse tracks that separate the lining from the casement cloth, and with too hot a sun or at night you can pull the lining across for complete protection. This idea isn't cheap because you are paying for the labor of making two separate pairs of draperies. The fact that casement cloths generally present a loose weave brings up fading, rotting and riding. As I have already noted, linen is the best protection in the world against rotting and riding, but it is a little weak in the dye department. Kept in the white range, however, it is an extremely long-wearing fiber that gives you a minimum of trouble, lends itself to a variety of intricate designs, and is a visual winner to boot. Its other problem (you've guessed it) is that it is expensive.

If you are not planning to live in your house at least ten years, you may not wish to invest much money in almost entire walls of draperies. There are many incredibly lovely open weaves made of other fibers. They probably will not rot until you are long gone, but riding could possibly be an early problem. Merely rehem those that ride. It doesn't take a genius to do it, just time. Accept it as a probability on buying fabrics with an open weave pattern. Any cloth with a knitted effect will stretch easily, as will some of the inexpensive open boucle weaves of rayon.

Be alert when choosing an unusual weave to drape your window. Some intricately woven textures are exquisite when you hold them in your hand. Beware! That subtle quality can disappear into the hanging folds. A less expensive, less interesting fabric often does as well because the detail of the intricate fabric does not always show up in the shadows of the window wall. Also watch the horizontal nub in casement cloths, which are usually added to instill a masculine quality. The see-through nature of the fabric can cause a dominating nub to perform as if it were a horizontal stripe.

For dressy fabrics, silk is the ultimate, but it soon rots in strong sunlight, so it should always be lined. Be wary of using the queen of fabrics on the south side of the house. Silk's shiny, dressy quality can be found in many less expensive synthetics, so it is no problem to find a substitute. As a result, you find that the antique satin for your living room costs less than the intricate casement cloth for your family room. Your husband may not appreciate it, but just explain to him that he is so lucky that he can purchase the dressier draperies so reasonably today. But watch out for acetate, it does not wear well by itself, but straightens out when combined with another fiber, such as rayon. Rayon itself rots less quickly in conjunction with other fibers. Unfortunately, an all-rayon drapery shrinks if it hangs over a heating vent.

In the lightweight sheer category, the list of synthetics and combinations which contain them grows longer every day. Popular for that weightless look are Dacron, Ninon, Zantrel, Bemberg, Polyester, Antron, Avril, Chromspun, Verel, and Fortisan. Even an acrylic fiber makes an appearance, looking like wool but less expensive. Since it is a fabric that burns readily, you can be quite sure the mills add other fibers to it. Beautiful, expensive mohair makes up fabrics that appear as if fairies have spun it, but if white it may yellow with age. Sad but true, it also costs more to dry clean than does the usual drapery fabric.

When you are choosing your drapery or sheer curtain fabric, bypass fiberglass. The tremendous advertising campaign that has been wasted over the years on this fabric makes you suspicious of the whole operation. Its faults far outweigh its good points; the outstanding complaint is that it hangs dreadfully, refusing to cooperate with pinch pleats. It is indeed the "drop out" of curtain materials. Nobody wants to sell it, and nobody wants to sew it since it sheds glass dust (a health hazard) and is most brittle (it can split in long slits). An excellent substitute for commercial purposes is Ravana-Verel. It has all the good qualities of fiberglass, it lacks dangerous dust particles, and it also hangs well.

There are three methods of dyeing fabrics. In synthetics, the dyes may be added in the liquid state. These fabrics therefore tend to be the most colorfast, although it is dangerous to make general statements about dyeing. Fibers or yarns are more often dyed before weaving. With a print, obviously, the dye is added after the weaving. This order of process, as you can see, would be less substantial because the dye cannot saturate the whole yarn.

The kind and intensity of dye used affect colorfastness, but almost all materials fade in varying degrees if exposed to the sun or washing. Perhaps the smart idea would be to select colors that fade in a mellow way. The colors used by nature—gray, brown, green, yellow, and orange—retain a pleasing appearance longer than colors of higher intensity. Mixtures, textures and prints do not become as listless as faded solid colors. Dark, solid colors quickly lose their richness and depth in the sun, and blue sometimes can be a particular problem. All this is not said to condemn dark or bright solid colors, but just to alert you to the fact that you will probably have to replace them sooner.

Consider the texture of your draperies in conjunction with the style of your room. Rich antique satin weaves are not for Early American family rooms. Rough burlap-textured linens are not ideal for dressy French living rooms. Prints, too, by their design, suggest formality and informality. A chintz is a delightful drapery fabric, so fresh and gay, with an additional bonus—dirt shakes off it. It can be formal or informal depending on the delicacy or intricacy of its design, although some patterns are hard to judge. A large bouquet of flowers in a hand-blocked English chintz can be anywhere from the middle range to dressy, but such rating is also true of some small patterns of French brocade. Glosheen designs are rarely dressy simply because the material is Glosheen. A practical buy, often guaranteed against most failings, and reasonable in price, Glosheen generally washes well. It is designed with budgeteers in mind.

Formality costs more than informality. Cotton prints usually settle for the middle-to-informal look. The fabric, unlike chintz with its slick appearance, is not the blue blood of the fabric line. A printed linen, however, is another thing. Linen has a richness about it because its interesting texture gives a certain depth to the design that is appealing. It can be almost dressy when the fiber is smooth and shiny, and most informal when rough and heavy. In this state it is marvelous with the velvet and leathers of the Renaissance periods. It gives character to an Early American interior, and it looks good with the English Queen Anne and Chippendale styles. In a contemporary design it is happy with Danish Modern.

To add to your list of helpful hints, I hope you realize that a natural bouquet of flowers is not compatible with the severe lines of any modern type of furniture. Another point—whole walls of a print are difficult. So remember that the smaller the window space is, the more successful the print will be, except for the miniature window, in which case we revert to plain fabric. When decorating, do not call attention to any abnormality in the size of a window. And avoid the horizontal stripes for your walls with draperies. Nothing could be less appealing.

Draperies hanging straight may seem dull to style seekers, but they serve their purpose and their timeless quality makes them answer to any occasion. Tied-back draperies are two-faced. With rich fabrics, they spell formality; with common fabrics, informality. A ruffle at the edge completes the cozy look even more. The cafe style drape is too bobtailed to be really formal. But, being adaptable, it works in a double tier, as a single perhaps crowned with a ruffle for a valance, or even with draperies, particularly when tied back.

See-through curtains, or sheers, came out of the mothballs a few years ago. What a comeback, from the simplest weaves to the most elaborate laces! Hanging straight or tied back in conjunction with draperies, sheers are sweeping the country.

Now is the time to speak of valances (to put the carpenter to work). Ruffles and box pleats belong to the informal styles, including Early American. Shaped valances of covered plywood belong with a later period such as American Colonial or eighteenth-century English. They need not necessarily be dressy to look right in almost any decor. Swag valances are elaborate and are at their best with the later

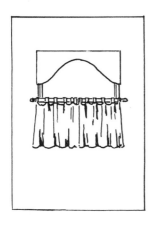

Cafe Drapery

French periods, English Regency, and Victorian. Swags, as well as shaped box valances, look fine with today's Italian provincial furniture. Sometimes a swag valance can have tails so long on both sides that draperies aren't needed at all. At times we see the two-color effect: the valance is one color, the drapery another. Or perhaps a print

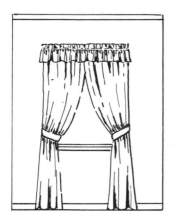

Informal

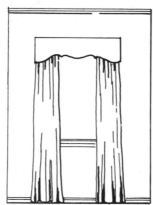

Formal

is used in conjunction with a plain fabric. I feel that the area is too small, the gift of unity of purpose disrupted too entirely, to make this division acceptable.

When traverse track and straight draperies are rejected for a more elaborate interpretation of drapery treatment, it becomes almost imperative to add a window shade, at least in rooms which for modesty's sake require a screen to separate them from the outside world. Most of the time this need is met by a white shade, but a shade can become so splendid that it takes over the whole function of a window treatment. Regular window shade material plus blackout fabrics now come in sweet pastels, strong heavy colors, masculine textures, and attractive stripes. The choice is up to you, and they are all so interesting that it may be a hard one to make.

Prints or textures can be laminated or plasticized to make stunning roller shades to match your room perfectly. For abnormally small windows in bathrooms, dormer windows in bedrooms, or the long narrow shaped windows found in contemporary homes, they are unobtrusive because they can so easily be rolled up out of the way.

For the masculine look, wooden loom (bamboo) shades are fabulous, but they do not provide complete blackout. Here is one material that looks correct running horizontally. The small strips of wood are unwieldy when placed vertically and are intensely unattractive in this position. Please do not have them made up this way because they break off at the ends too easily when used as draperies. They are somewhat costly, and I know you will be unhappy with them in the long run.

There are also Roman shades made of material such as linen and that go up and down on the same principle as the venetian blind. Colored bands often run vertically on these somewhat complicated window coverings in order to hide, for one thing, their mechanical parts. They are extremely flattering and in high style; nevertheless, if they are located on a window where they are busily zipped up and down the material bunches in a sloppy manner when up, and shows regularly spaced horizontal wrinkles when down. For the apartment house window that hides an ugly back alley, they are great.

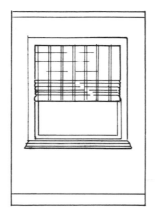 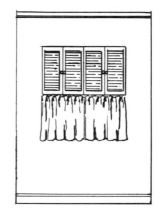

Roman Shade

Last but not least are shutters, window coverings that are heartily endorsed by suburbanites. More architectual than decorative, they are costly but will last until the house is knocked down. Attractive by themselves, they can also be used in conjunction with draperies. But watch your sill space: if the window sills are not deep enough for the shutters to fold neatly and completely when open, they can interfere with the draperies' functioning.

I have never been fond of just half a shutter. When placed on the top side of the window, it appears to be too heavy for the drapery on the bottom half. Its use on just the lower half is an improvement, but it still has a sliced-off-in-the-middle look. Very informal in character, it may do for a kitchen with a pretty ruffled valance above. It's far better to go the whole way, though, and, with a deep enough sill, shutters create a marvelous old world atmosphere. If the wood is stained, except when matched in paneled rooms of eighteenth-century style, they should be placed in the informal column. Painted, they can look formal or informal, and they look gay indeed if they are painted a bright color to match a scheme in a bedroom or bath.

The price of installation seems excessive to many husbands, but believe me, installation is an extremely difficult procedure except for the most competent do-it-yourself husband. Try to convince your hero that he has met his master and should bow to the expert in the field. The double tier shutter refuses to behave no matter who installs it.

Carpets and rugs are always a scarey buy because they involve so much money. It is wise not to buy a shoddy rug, but you can also overdo it and purchase one that will last longer than you need it. There is no real purpose in buying a carpet that will last thirty years for a house in which you are going to live for only five years. Nature's fiber, wool, is king probably because its resilience is so great. It is scarce and therefore expensive, it is the most beautiful fiber for rugs, it offers the most variety of effects, it cleans well, it shows soil the least and its wear will depend on its price or the amount of wool in the rug. Woven in a tight weave and thick, like Oriental rugs, it lasts for generations.

Synthetics come and go. All the synthetics I know about are imitations of wool. A few, such as tough wearing nylon, have been on the market for years, and we know now what to expect of them. There is no doubt that nylon is successful in a shag weave, the most popular style today with females. Most synthetics wear longer but look worse than wool if the same amount is used per square inch; the dyes are more colorfast; they clean easier when new, but get dirty faster and are cheaper. They have their faults. They neither look nor feel quite like the real thing, and in time they tend to mat or knot or flatten; with age, they may present an impossible cleaning problem because of ugly stains. And don't forget that colorfast acrylic fiber (the prettiest synthetic) is combustible unless other chemicals have been added. The polyesters (stamped with many trade names just to confuse you) are supposed to resist stain and dirt the best. They are not so resilient as was first expected and look well only in cut pile. If you do not intend to live in one place for long, or are on a budget, synthetics are a good buy. Just don't buy a brand new synthetic on the market that is being pushed to the limit by an expensive advertising campaign. Its problems still need to be worked out.

With a cut pile in plain colors we can achieve as dressy a background as is necessary for any style, but it is broad enough to be informal as well. Deep, shaggy piles, although masculine and sloppy, are luxurious enough to provide a background for the most formal rooms. Yet a smooth cut pile is still best for a truly royal look. Tweed in a cut pile is not particularly dressy, and a looped pile tends toward informality. Combine the loop pile with a tweed pattern and you have a very informal look indeed.

Patterned rugs are complicated to manufacture and are most often woven in wool. Even Early American and simple Danish Modern braided rugs are best in wool. A few years ago, hooked rugs were limited to Early American or French Provincial decor, but they are now becoming so popular as a handicraft item that area rugs are in; the design itself dictates what background they best fit.

French Aubusson and Savonnerie rugs tend to be dressy. The simpler Oriental—the Chinese style—looks good with Oriental furniture, naturally, as well as with eighteenth-century American and English styles and Modern. The Near East Orientals have a timelessness about them that have made them favorites for generations, and I am sure they will never go out of favor. Costly, long-wearing, practical for the roughest of family life, they can follow you wherever you go. Take their colors into consideration as you decorate, and they can be a delight to you always.

Area rugs are well named. Defining areas is exactly their purpose. You do not walk on area rugs in order to go to and from a room, but rather to go into a section and sit down to pursue such pleasures as conversation or eating. Ridiculous in a tiny room, which really deserves scatter rugs or a room-size rug to answer its purpose, they are great for large rooms in which they can break up that wide prairie look (which wall-to-wall carpeting can create) into islands of interests. It is sensible to leave at least twenty-four inches between rugs to insure a decent path for walking. People do not enjoy having one foot up on a rug, particularly if it is thick, and the other foot on the floor as they walk through a room.

When you have more than one area rug in a room, be sure you don't have a set of twins. The resulting sameness results in boredom. Serve up some variety. If the patterns match, vary the size; if the sizes match, combine a pattern with a plain weave. If it is Orientals you favor, different designs almost always go well with each other.

Since area rugs cut up space, and since the beauty of wall-to-wall carpeting is the quiet extension of space, it does seem ridiculous to place an area rug on top of wall-to-wall carpeting. I am rarely in favor of a double floor covering. One of the problems is that since you are so well supplied with a rug by the carpet you think you can get away with a postage stamp-size area rug, but you can't. The effect is awful. Picture instead a bare floor and regulate the size of your area rug correctly. The furniture of a section should completely stand on an area rug, or at least the rug should come up to the furniture's edge. How I hate to see the coffee table standing knee-deep on a tiny shaggy rug, like an island in the middle of the ocean. But double floor covering does not mean padding, which is always a good idea: it lengthens the wear, the rug looks and feels more luxurious, and it keeps scatter rugs from slipping.

Carpets for the kitchen? I guess I am a bit too old-fashioned for this sort of thing. My personal belief is that the fiber has not been invented that can take the place of tile. I am still waiting for the invention of the perfect tile—soft under foot, with a pleasant sheen that never has to be polished. Until that comes about, I'll settle for vinyl. I can't always stop and mop thoroughly, and the thought of a raw egg slowly seeping through my kitchen carpet as I rush off somewhere for a three-hour conference is more than I can bear.

By now you should have a clearer view of what the market is all about and of how you can select from all that is available to you. You should be ready to relax and enjoy the excitement that goes with putting a house together. If you still feel apprehensive about giving birth to ideas, or if you still lack confidence in your ability to be different and to display good taste at the same time, perhaps my last chapter, which describes finished rooms and shows their floor plans, will provide enough of a guide to boost your confidence so that you can select the right material to make your home both fashionable and livable.

৯ 7

Ideas for a Designing Woman

The following pages describe each type of room found in most American homes. This is not one house, because the rooms show no continuity. Rather, its purpose is to give you the feeling of a finished room and some ideas that you may not find in every house up and down your block. It might be better said in photographs, but these rooms do not actually exist. Some, like the living room, are expensively decorated, and some, like the family room, are not.

The entrance hall has extremely narrow door-height windows on each side of the front door. They are covered with bright yellow sheers pulled taut from top to bottom. The wallpaper, the main feature, is charcoal with huge, stylish, individual yellow roses surrounded by delicate flower sprays in white and an occasional bee, bird and butterfly. The wood floor is kept highly polished and has a rug in buttercup yellow. The same rose, outlined in charcoal, creates a border around the rug. The wall on the bench side of the hall is completely mirrored; along with the darkness of the background of the wallpaper, it tends to give this hall great depth, which most halls lack.

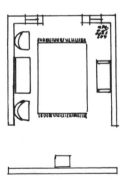

A bamboo chest against the wallpaper is antiqued in yellow, and above it is a large painting, Flemish in feeling with a dark background. It creates a peaceful look of a garden in bloom, with birds, bees, turtles, snails, rabbits, and the like. This painting contains not only a great deal of yellow, but other colors as well. Side chairs with a Chinese lattice pattern for their backs have bright yellow cushions for seats. Over the side chair, mirrored sconces add a glittering effect.

A grandfather's clock opposite the front door greets the guests, and the bench against the mirror is upholstered in a yellow lattice pattern. A branched, treelike potted plant stands in the corner by the door and helps to create a feeling of formality. A plywood screen jutting out

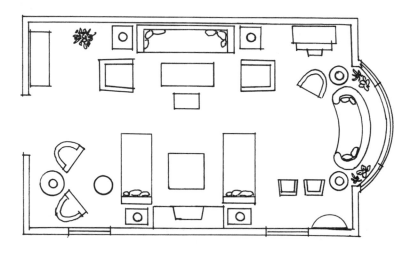

from the living room wall is covered with the same wallpaper as the hall in order to give a sense of flow. A chandelier of charcoal-painted wrought iron designed with entwining yellow roses gaily puts the finishing touches to this chic entrance.

Here is a capital living room for formal entertaining with plenty of room for everyone. The furniture combines the best of Louis XV and XVI with English Regency to create a pleasing balance of curves and straight lines. The walls and wall-to-wall carpeting are the palest sea green. The draperies are a somewhat darker green of heavy satin topped by curved plywood-covered valances. The large sofa against the main wall is upholstered in the same fabric as the draperies, and on the two chaise lounges flanking the fireplace is an especially beautiful rich tapestry in a Chinese dragon design of greens and light gray roses. The two upholstered chairs by the sofa carry a wide stripe combining the pinks and greens. Soft old rose is found on the two small Louis XV bergeres near the entrance, and the little curved late Regency love seat in the window repeats the rose in a medallion-patterned damask. The curved upholstered chair near the window adds some character to the room by being upholstered in a deeply grayed forest green velvet cover. The two Louis XVI wooden armchairs opposite have upholstered mulberry seats and backs. Hanging flat against the wall above the large sofa is a Chinese screen with all of the colors in the room plus silver.

The bench on the far side of the large coffee table is in a maroon brocade with tiny, soft pink flowers and green leaves. A Regency chair drawn up to the breakfront desk is pale pink. The room is splendid with a great deal of shining silver and crystal, such as a crystal chandelier hanging in the center, silver candelabra on the mantle, and silver urn-shaped lamps by the large sofa. Along with the silver accessories, handsome pieces of Chinese porcelain in multi-colored patterns are appropriate.

On available wall spaces hang large scenic oil paintings of woods and fields to give warmth to the room. High, potted plants are placed at both ends of the bay to introduce the eye to the landscape outside. To the right of the sofa is a pedestal holding a magnificent bouquet of flowers. A stereo by the entrance plays quiet classical music to make the scene even more serene. With a fire blazing in the fireplace, a sense of peace and quiet pervades the whole room even though the color scheme contains sharp contrasts.

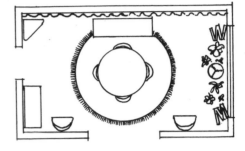

Here is an attractive contemporary dining room. The buffet sits against a wall covered with gathered fabric printed with orange colored winter trees on a white background. The wall of glass is covered with shuttered, folding floor-to-ceiling doors painted the same orange as the trees. On the floor in front of the window are numerous potted plants. Centered above the plants, a bird cage swings from the ceiling for another bright touch. The chairs with gold leather seats are pushed up to a sophisticated center pedestal table. The orange and gold rug is thickly tufted.

By the wall toward the kitchen is a mobile server that can help out with refreshments served to guests in the living room. A tripod in the corner holds a display of modern glass objects. The chandelier is modern, a round globe of shiny brass that emits light dramatically top and bottom. Above the server is a loud abstract painting filled with the colors of the room. The effect is gay and cheerful, matching the bright garden scene on the patio outside the wall of glass.

Family rooms generally become a catchall for hand-me-downs and early marriage purchases. In order to make a really long sofa, it must consist of two straight parts of a sectional group with no inner arms.

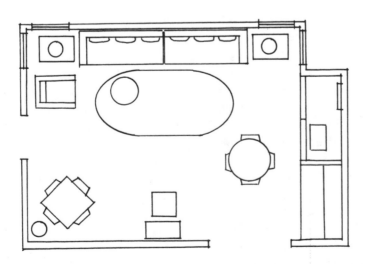

Dad's lounge chair is a matching piece. All of them are upholstered in oxblood vinyl plastic. The many soft pillows on the sofa have been covered in a fabric that is printed in a design resembling an old quilt. The walls are white except for the sofa wall, which is paneled in a dark finish and sports a collection of samplers. A braided oval rug is done in the multicolors of the pillows, yet has plenty of dark red to match the vinyl plastic. It sits on white tile in front of the sofa. The coffee table is small in order to allow plenty of free floor space.

The heavy, large end tables hold solid wood, candlestick-based lamps with natural linen shades. Directly across the room is the television in back of a square ottoman covered in dark blue vinyl plastic. To the left, a rugged, dual purpose game table with a flip top can serve for extra dining or for informal buffets and as a pattern-cutting table for mother. Around the table sit ladder-back chairs of moderate height with wide, slightly curved slats for comfort and with tied-on cushions of the same fabric as the sofa pillows. The corner windows are handsomely dressed with natural linen draperies trimmed in a braid of dark red and in another braid of dark blue. The large family bulletin board hangs on the wall by the game table. The young children's play table, about coffee table height and of white Formica, has four Mexican child's chairs, rich with splashy, painted patterns.

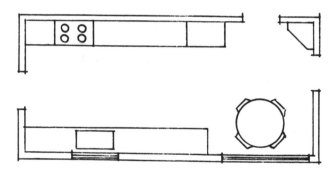

The storage space nearest the kitchen entrance consists of deep open shelves for toys, and the storage space on the side nearest the sofa is a closed affair with folding doors. It holds drawers, a kneehole section with the portable sewing machine above, and a drop-down ironing board at the far section. Lined with peg board, it keeps all the necessities for sewing within easy reach. Indirect lighting insures even lighting. Most surfaces are washable, down to the zipped-on pillows and seat covers. Only the reversible rug has to be dry cleaned every other year. A minimum of work keeps this room shipshape for smooth family sailing.

The kitchen can look as fresh as a lettuce leaf. The ceiling affects a tent look by being painted white with lines that are lettuce green in color; extending from the corners, they converge at the middle.

A dropped ceiling that meets the tops of the cupboards looks attractive painted in an outline of scallops in the same green. Where the two windows are located at the sink and at the breakfast nook, plywood valances extend over the window space to continue the same

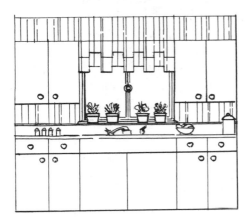

scallop design without a break. The draperies of white sail cloth are tied back and are trimmed with a lettuce green band. For privacy, white shades with the repeating green trim fill the bill. On the floor a green and white terrazzo tile is a practical covering, or a white Spanish tile design would be more exciting, depending on how often you like to mop the vinyl floor. The lower cupboards are painted lettuce green with the upper cupboards and Formica counter tops in white.

The dining table and chairs are a fancy design in wrought iron, painted lettuce green, and for a change of pace the seats are covered in daffodil yellow. In the corner stands an old corner cupboard antiqued in white with the back walls in lettuce green showing an interesting display of white and bright yellow china. Last but not least, the whole kitchen is tied together by a hand-printed, vinyl-coated paper portraying crisp green vegetables wherever the plaster presents itself. The paper has a canvas backing and thus is washable. All the appliances are in white. In a row on the sill by the sink, white-potted geraniums grow profusely in the warm sunshine. In a kitchen such as this any hot dish can be cooly handled.

For mother and father in a traditional house, we present a room done in the elegant eighteenth-century style that has grace and beauty yet solidarity that both can appreciate. Wallpaper and draperies match, but there is wallpaper on the bed wall only. This trick attracts attention to the bed and helps lessen the long look of the room. The draperies reach the floor and are capped by a regal swag valance. The print has a soft blue background with white flowers and touches of turquoise as well as Kelly green. Since the background of the paper is blue, the other three walls are painted matching blue.

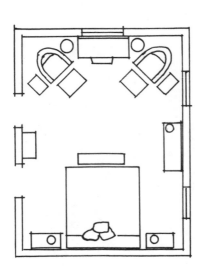

A bench at the foot of the bed also helps shorten the look of the room. A mahogany double dresser fills the space between windows. On each side of the bed is a console table loaded with all the articles that make lounging in bed before lights out a pleasant pastime. The lamps have pure white bases, shaped as vases. Here also are pretty bouquets of flowers in season, and green plants at other times.

Since the home is filled with the noisy sound of lively teenagers, mom and dad like to escape to their room in the evening. Thus at one side is a portable television and at another wall dad solves left-over business problems at a desk in a group with two comfortable lounge chairs and ottomans. The matching chairs and ottomans are upholstered in a soft turquoise, while the desk chair is in Kelly green. Two candlestick floor lamps make reading by the desk easy. Both chairs are flanked by magazine racks and one chair sports mom's mending box. The four-poster queen-size bed has a quilted, pure white bedspread and three pillows of two values of blue and one of turquoise. The bench at the foot of the bed is smartly covered in a narrow white, blue and turquoise stripe. A large Aubusson rug woven mostly in blue and turquoise almost fills the room. It is a gracious room, but thoroughly livable.

In order to design something a little different for your eleven-year-old girl's room, we have added some carpentry work with built-ins.

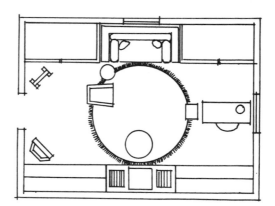

Since the French style is so feminine, we choose this style for her, but decide to have the furniture in natural walnut instead of the usual girl's choice of white. Two closets jut out into the room, making an alcove for her bed. A French daybed has equally high headboard, footboard and back. Here are bolsters and a group of pillows. The wallpaper matches the patterned fabric, which has a white background well covered with a pale apricot flower. The fabric is quilted for durability, and the covers on all the furniture are removable for easy cleaning.

The three windows have window shades laminated of the same material. The ceiling is dropped by the bed to make a true alcove, and from it ruffled draperies tie back at the closet edge. The two free windows have tied-back ruffled draperies that reach to the floor, while the window in the alcove is covered merely by the window shade. The floor is tiled with a pale apricot vinyl for easy maintenance because this gal is an artist. In one corner of the room, on the diagonal, an easel is set up. In the other corner by the closet is a full-length, old-fashioned mirror set in a frame and on legs. The large round rug has a deep pile and is white with fringe all around. There is plenty of space on it for visiting little girls and their bed rolls. There will probably be a fight over the bed, though, and lots will have to be drawn.

The lady's writing table coming out from the wall has probably a few more years to function as a desk, at which time it may change into being a table for cutting out dress patterns and holding the sewing machine. Above it, a French Provincial hanging shelf is loaded with horse statues because this little girl occupies herself on weekends with riding. Her latest artistic endeavors are pinned to her bulletin board on the built-in chest wall above the stereo. Her old closet was ripped out to make way for a row of drawers with bookcases on both sides of the wide space given to the bulletin board. The wide chest top takes care of the stereo and records. In front of the stereo is a round ottoman on casters, which is covered with a chintz slip cover and skirt. An antiqued apricot wooden bench by the side of the desk also has casters and can move over to the bed as an occasional coffee table with the ottoman joining the group for extra seating space. A quaint Toleware floor lamp serves for lighting by her bed. Only a sweet little doll of a girl should be allowed to have a room like this.

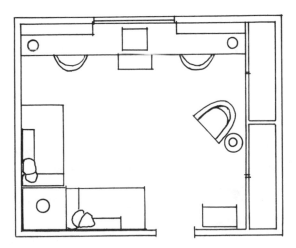

Here we have a teenage boy's room for two brothers. The walls are dark brown, but with white wood work. On the floor is a wall-to-wall, thick, looped pile, white rug sprinkled with black and brown tufts for practicality. A long white Formica shelf stretches along the whole side of the window wall, and on each end drawers are built to the floor. White wooden bookcases rise from the shelf to the ceiling on both sides of the large window. The window covering is a dark finished, wooden loom slat shade. A typewriter table with casters for moving it around the room sits under the shelf desk centered between two comfortable Danish Modern chairs. This table is also topped with white Formica and can be used for the typewriter or for games such as chess, or it can be moved across the room to be used as a coffee table in front of the beds. This sort of table might have many uses. The desk shelf is more than broad enough to take the stereo that sits in the middle. The records are conveniently stacked vertically on the desk section below the first shelf for books. The high shelves take the leftovers of their earlier days of collecting and model building. Naugahyde, in a zebra stripe, looks great on the chair seats. A modern upholstered chair is covered in a heavy black tweed, and the fabric on the two beds, including the long bolsters and large pillows at the head, is a handsome plaid of brown, black and white. By the chair is a sturdy modern tray lamp of black with touches of brass.

The corner table repeats the white Formica. On it is a far-out lamp with lots of brass. In the only free corner is a high chest of drawers. This is enough for the room because the boys also have chests built into their closets. A bulletin board, probably for pictures of girls at this point, stays above the chest. The boys are ski nuts, so the walls around the bed are loaded with loud blue ski posters.

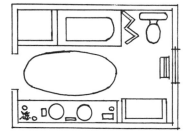

Let's have some fun with the bathroom. This room does it with colorful, inexpensive prints from the Grandma Moses collection. The wooden frames are antiqued to look like pewter. The prints hang all over the bathroom, high and low without formal arrangement. The walls and cupboards are paneled in wood resembling the sides of an old barn. The floor, covered with red brick tile, has a bright green hooked rug on it. Between the tub and the toilet is placed a low screen of the same rustic wood as the walls.

The double-tier cafe draperies at the window, the seat cover on the bench, and the shower curtain are all in the strong blue checked material of the old kitchen table cloth. An old wagon seat is substituted for a bench and is painted in screaming yellow. Under the window, a purple magazine rack holds the latest, or perhaps it should be the oldest, reading material. A wooden shelf, painted orange, hangs over the toilet for a display of milk-glass bottles. The towels are multicolored stripes to tie, along with the prints, the many colors together. Over each sink a pewter-framed mirror with pewter sconces on each side is used to increase the look of age. The cabinet door-knobs are pewter. No one is allowed in unless he is wearing blue jeans.

You have seen decorator samples of the major rooms. Now it is your turn to be at home with decorating. A handsome color scheme, a practical room arrangement all wrapped up in good taste with consideration for that lived-in look, should make your home an unqualified success for all concerned. Relax, and enjoy the excitement and pleasure that go along with decorating. Then, I am sure, the results will be comfortable, happy and beautiful.